The Therapist's Secrets

The Academic and Clinical Journeys

THE WORLD OF PSYCHOLOGY: THERAPEUTIC, RELATIONAL, TEACHING

AMI ROKACH - SERIES EDITOR –
THE CENTER FOR ACADEMIC STUDIES,
OR YEHUDA, ISRAEL
YORK UNIVERSITY, TORONTO, CANADA
WALDEN UNIVERSITY, MN, USA

Sex, Love and Laughter
Ami Rokach and Itzhak Zahy Ben Zion
2015. ISBN: 978-1-63483-258-8

Victim Victorious: From Fire to Phoenix
Marie-Claire Patron, and Stephen S. Holden (Editors)
2015. ISBN: 978-1-63482-216-9

The Therapist's Secrets: The Academic and Clinical Journeys
Ami Rokach
2014. ISBN: 978-1-63117-603-6 (Hardcover)
2015. ISBN: 978-1-63483-807-8

THE WORLD OF PSYCHOLOGY: THERAPEUTIC,
RELATIONAL, TEACHING

THE THERAPIST'S SECRETS

THE ACADEMIC AND CLINICAL JOURNEYS

AMI ROKACH, PHD

New York

Copyright © 2015 by Nova Science Publishers, Inc.

All rights reserved. No part of this book may be reproduced, stored in a retrieval system or transmitted in any form or by any means: electronic, electrostatic, magnetic, tape, mechanical photocopying, recording or otherwise without the written permission of the Publisher.

We have partnered with Copyright Clearance Center to make it easy for you to obtain permissions to reuse content from this publication. Simply navigate to this publication's page on Nova's website and locate the "Get Permission" button below the title description. This button is linked directly to the title's permission page on copyright.com. Alternatively, you can visit copyright.com and search by title, ISBN, or ISSN.

For further questions about using the service on copyright.com, please contact:
Copyright Clearance Center
Phone: +1-(978) 750-8400   Fax: +1-(978) 750-4470   E-mail: info@copyright.com

NOTICE TO THE READER

The Publisher has taken reasonable care in the preparation of this book, but makes no expressed or implied warranty of any kind and assumes no responsibility for any errors or omissions. No liability is assumed for incidental or consequential damages in connection with or arising out of information contained in this book. The Publisher shall not be liable for any special, consequential, or exemplary damages resulting, in whole or in part, from the readers' use of, or reliance upon, this material. Any parts of this book based on government reports are so indicated and copyright is claimed for those parts to the extent applicable to compilations of such works.

Independent verification should be sought for any data, advice or recommendations contained in this book. In addition, no responsibility is assumed by the publisher for any injury and/or damage to persons or property arising from any methods, products, instructions, ideas or otherwise contained in this publication.

This publication is designed to provide accurate and authoritative information with regard to the subject matter covered herein. It is sold with the clear understanding that the Publisher is not engaged in rendering legal or any other professional services. If legal or any other expert assistance is required, the services of a competent person should be sought. FROM A DECLARATION OF PARTICIPANTS JOINTLY ADOPTED BY A COMMITTEE OF THE AMERICAN BAR ASSOCIATION AND A COMMITTEE OF PUBLISHERS.

Additional color graphics may be available in the e-book version of this book.

Library of Congress Cataloging-in-Publication Data

The therapist's secrets : the academic and clinical journeys / Author: Ami Rokach (Dept. of Psychology, The Center for Academic Studies, Or Yehuda, Israel).
    pages cm. -- (The world of psychology: therapeutic, relational, teaching)
    Includes index.
    ISBN 978-1-63483-807-8 (softcover)
 1. Rokach, Ami. 2. Psychotherapists--Biography. 3.   Clinical psychologists--Biography. 4. Psychotherapists--Training of. 5. Psychotherapy--Vocational guidance. I. Rokach, Ami.
    RC438.6.R65A3 2014
    616.89'14092--dc23
                                                            [B]
                                                            2014009816

Published by Nova Science Publishers, Inc. † New York

The bumblebee

Some time ago a group of aeronautical engineers decided to study the bumblebee. They measured its wingspan, computed body weight, examined its oversized fuselage and concluded that there was no rational reason why a bumblebee can take off or land safely. Of course, the bumblebee doesn't know this, so it goes ahead and flies anyway!

Anonymous

Dedicated to

Reg Reynolds, my beloved supervisor
Ken Scapinello, my dear friend and colleague
Milada Disman, a wonderful soul
Marty Resnick, my very dear teacher and friend
David Teplin, my dear friend and supporter
My Love, Natalie
and my dear Benny, whose journey inspired this book.

My special thanks to Gwenelle Philibert,
who helped with typing and editing the book,
and to Doreen Ioannou, Marlene Almeda,
Nicole Mitchell, and Geri Venegas,
who read the manuscript and made many comments
that, I believe, improved it.

CONTENTS

Foreword		xiii
	Raymond J. Trybus	
Part 1: Focused, Determined, Committed		**1**
Chapter 1	The Beginning	3
	The Obstacle Course Begins	*3*
	Psychology: Choosing with the Heart	*6*
Chapter 2	Choosing a University and Getting In	9
Chapter 3	Attending Undergraduate School	13
Chapter 4	Lessons I Learned in Undergraduate School	17
	Assignments and Writing Papers	*18*
	More and Less Interesting Courses	*19*
	Professors	*19*
	Learning, Performing, Enjoying	*20*
Chapter 5	Applying and Getting into Graduate School	21
Chapter 6	Graduate School	23
Chapter 7	Life after the Degree	27
Chapter 8	Becoming a Clinical Psychologist	31
	Supervision	*33*
	What I Have Learned in School and in Supervision	*34*

Part 2: Being a Psychologist: Healing, Teaching, and Researching		**37**
Chapter 9	Research	**39**
	Research is Almost Always More Complicated, Unforeseen, and Takes Longer Than Planned	*39*
	What to Research: Finding an Area That 'Needs' Your Contribution	*40*
	Publishing is Not for the Faint of Heart	*41*
Chapter 10	Teaching	**43**
Chapter 11	Psychotherapy	**47**
	Why do People Choose Psychotherapy as Their Profession?	*47*
	Approaching Psychotherapy	*48*
	My Model of Psychotherapy	*49*
	Therapy = Acquiring Choice	*52*
	A Rule of Thumb	*53*
	To Be, or Not To Be Someone's Therapist	*54*
Chapter 12	The Process of Psychotherapy	**57**
	Initiating	*57*
	Navigating Through the Client's Life	*59*
	Our Values – Do We Ignore Them?	*60*
	Therapy as a Microcosm of Reality	*61*
	Reframing: The Delicious Little Deviancy	*61*
	The Therapeutic Relationship	*63*
	Some Observations on Therapeutic Relations	*64*
	Intimacy in Therapy	*67*
	Fellow Travelers	*69*
	Support and Empower the Client	*69*
	Therapy is Not Just for the Office	*70*
	Checking the Client's Experience in Therapy	*71*
	"Do You Ever Think of Me Between Sessions?"	*72*
	To Admit or Not to Admit to Your Mistakes	*72*
	The Uniqueness of Each Client	*73*
	The Client, Here and Now	*74*
	Self-Reflection	*74*
	The Promise and Problems of Transference	*75*
	Therapist's Self-Disclosure	*76*
	What and When to Self-Disclose?	*77*

	Freedom: A Duty and a Goal	*77*
	Assuming Responsibility	*78*
	A Silenced Client	*79*
	It is Easy to 'Destroy' a Client	*80*
	Dreams	*81*
	Occupational Hazards	*82*
Epilogue	Personal Growth and Richness of Experience	**85**
Appendix A	Counseling Psychology: Teaching the Theories Experientially	**87**
	Introduction	*87*
	Structure of Class Meetings	*91*
	Course Evaluation	*94*
	The First Meeting	*97*
	Every Dysfunction is Functional	*104*
	The Rest of the Semester	*106*
	The Therapeutic Relationship	*109*
	The First In-Class Counseling Session	*115*
	Conclusion	*119*
Appendix B	How to Make the Most of this Class, or ROPES	**123**
References		**125**
About the Author		**127**
Index		**129**

FOREWORD

One of the many significant topics addressed in learning to become a psychologist and perform psychotherapy is the question of psychologist self-disclosure. Yes? No? When? How much? About what? With whom? Under what conditions and with what purpose? A basic tenet is that self-disclosure is done in measured doses, and only for the purpose of advancing the client's or patient's interests, not out of the psychologist's need to disclose.

My initial thought was: "Thank goodness that in this volume Ami Rokach is not our therapist, but our colleague and fellow traveler, so that we are able to have the benefit of his extensive self-disclosure in this very personal communication." Upon further thought, though, I think that Ami has actually decided that our interests as his readers – students, potential students, and maybe fellow travelers along similar paths – would be well served by extensive personal disclosure, and so that is what he has given us.

Ami has shared what might be thought of as a compilation of "letters to home" with us, written at intervals during his own journey to and through the field of psychology. Developmental theorists have talked about the generative stage, in which a key developmental task is "paying it forward" to the next generation. In this short work, that is what you will see – an experienced psychologist doing a life review and sharing the benefits of his experiences and lessons learned with those who are contemplating a similar journey.

So many times in the course of these pages, I found myself thinking or saying, "Ahh yes, I remember that feeling/thought/experience/worry/hope/fear," and realizing that I had long forgotten or repressed many of those episodes in my own life journey until reading his heartfelt prose. Then I realized that, clever psychologist that he is, he has been using his own self-disclosure precisely in what he judged to be in the best interest of us, his readers, in order to help us bring to awareness what might be hidden. For those of you who, like Ami, who are well along on your life journey, I invite you to share that same sense of "aha!", that sense of recognition.

For those of you who are just beginning the journey, or perhaps contemplating whether to even buy a ticket on this train, I invite you to delve into this volume as you might into a travel guide to a foreign yet enticing destination, to help you decide whether to take the trip.

But the train trip metaphor is not the right one, as Ami makes clear. Trains stay on already-laid-out tracks, reaching their destination via a clearly defined path, with predictable stops and crossing guard mechanisms to keep potential obstructions off the tracks.

Ami's journey has been more like a memorable airplane ride: patches of rough air and sometimes heart-stopping turbulence; grand panoramic vistas followed by detours around potentially dangerous thunderheads; rapid changes of altitude that make us doubt that our hearts and stomachs really do have relatively fixed locations in our insides; changing visibility conditions so that the underlying terrain sometimes fades out of sight. Will we find the landing strip when the fog rolls in? Dare we trust the instruments and the skill of the pilots to bring us to a destination that we can recognize as somewhere we wanted to go? Will we really need to know how to use the oxygen masks and remember all the instructions in the safety briefing?

Ami's life flight did eventually find clear skies and smooth air, and he reassures us that ours can as well. The memories of all that transpired on the way to that smooth flying only serve to make the eventual arrival only sweeter and more appreciated.

So, fasten your seatbelts, put your tray tables in the upright and locked position, and focus your attention on your safety instruction card: this marvelous little volume. Remember to turn off your cell phones and other electronic devices, and focus your attention on Ami, who is up front there giving us explanations and demonstrations from his depth of experience with an often unpredictable flight path, as well as with the satisfaction of a journey that captures our full energy and makes us realize that we are capable of reaching destinations we were afraid to envision at take-off.

Thanks, Ami. In this book you've proven to be a great adventure-travel guide, and a great salesperson for one of the best fields known to humanity. I hope the skies are clear for the remaining legs of your journey, and we'll be right behind you!

Raymond J. Trybus, Ph.D.
Program Director, Clinical Psychology
School of Psychology, College of Social and Behavioral Sciences
Walden University
Minneapolis MN 55401
April, 2014

PART 1: FOCUSED, DETERMINED, COMMITTED

This part of the book will detail my journey through undergraduate and graduate school, what it took to get in, and how I learned to survive and thrive, without utilizing 'politics'. I am certain that my experience is similar to many others who study at university, and therefore I think that the bits of advice and wisdom that I have collected may be helpful to those who are already, or are planning, to attend university.

> The best way to predict the future – is to create it!
>
> Allan Kay

Chapter 1

THE BEGINNING

Do what you can, with what you have, where you are.
                                        Theodore Roosevelt

THE OBSTACLE COURSE BEGINS

"And what will you do if you do not get in *this* time?" asked my neighbor, who was aware of my burning desire to study psychology on the one hand, and the low motivation that universities had shown towards accepting me, two years in a row. I was startled, looked at her, and shared with her that I had no 'plan B'. I was going to study psychology!

The year was 1965. Almost 50 years ago, people did not usually attend psychotherapy or openly admitted to emotional issues, or, God forbid, that there may be anything that they could not handle by themselves. So, naturally, my parents' friend asked me, "How will you make a living being a psychologist? Who needs one, anyways?" In response, I related to him what my father had taught me since childhood, and later during adolescence when I was contemplating my future: "It is less important what you do," he said, "but how you do it. If you will be good at whatever you decide to do, you'll never starve." Today, 50 years later, I can attest to the accuracy of that observation. Most people may want money and a lot of it, and 'not starving' may not be what they are after, but what my father taught me indicated that it was up to me to determine what my life would be like, what I would choose to learn, and how I would practice it. Strive to excel is the message, and if you do your best (which is the utmost that anyone can do), life, financially and in other ways, will hopefully be good.

As I was growing up, and especially during my teens, I repeatedly heard how "easy and pleasant it is to speak with you." In liking interpersonal connection, being intrigued to discover how 'people tick', and enjoying listening to others, psychology seemed to be my destiny. While I knew that psychology was for me, I needed to discover whether I was right for psychology – in the eyes of the available universities, that is. Fortunately, in North America, we now have multiple options and academic institutions. Today, it is almost a given that if your grades are not terrible and you can pay, then you can get accepted into one undergraduate school at least – maybe not to the university that's your first choice, and not near your home, but you will get in. Five decades ago, in Israel (where I was born and raised), things were different. There were only three universities in the country and less than 10% of those who applied were accepted into psychology, which was right behind medicine in their requirements and had stringent expectations of applicants. Not only were we, the hopeful psychologists-to-be, expected to have very high grades, but our ability to 'walk on water' was taken for granted. Letters of reference were required and were to be very flattering. The infamous 'psychometric exam', a comprehensive test not unlike the Graduate Record Examination (GRE), had to be passed with flying colors by all those who wanted to enter the kingdom of psychology. My high school grades left a lot to be desired and I had some problems finding 'respected figures' who would write impressive letters for me. So I undertook the psychometric exam being quite unsure of myself, wondering whether I was actually cut out to become one of what then seemed to me to be the elite students who went to university. My heart skipped several beats when I received a letter from the psychology department at Tel Aviv University. Shaking, I opened the envelope and I was flooded with joy and appreciation, but felt anxious as well. I was invited for a personal interview, which would be the deciding factor as to whether I would become a psychology student. In North America, you *may* be called for an interview – or be interviewed over the phone – when you apply for Masters or Ph.D. programs. But at the time, Israel in the 1960s sifted carefully through the applicants who wanted to study psychology.

As the interview day approached, I remember my anxiety reaching heights and intensities I never knew it could rise to, and I remember looking at people around me and thinking to myself, "Man! Can't you be a plumber, a bus driver, or a store keeper, and do away with your ego and self-esteem being repeatedly put to the test?!" But then, I am 'wired' in such a way that once I decide to go for something, I will not voluntarily stop, like a Duracell Bunny of sorts. So I arrived for the interview, being convinced that my pounding heart and sweaty forehead would betray my anxiety. The interview was such an important factor in my attempt to gain entry into psychology and was preceded by a lot of reading about the field, while preparing for the expected question: "Why do you wish to become a psychologist?" Very quickly, I found out that 'they' had outsmarted me. The department chair and the undergraduate director who interviewed me started to speak with me about my life to that point, never getting to the expected question for which I was so prepared to answer. Instead, one of them suddenly asked me, "What makes you happy?" At that moment, I did not have what it takes for a quick comeback, which could have paved my way to being one of the blessed ones who were accepted. Instead, I was silent, caught off guard, imagining my shame when I would later tell all those who knew of my desire to study psychology and doubted that I was 'university material' that I was indeed a flop. Seeing my distress, the undergraduate director then offered, "Let's look at the other side of the coin: tell us, please, what upsets you." To this day, I believe that it must have been a higher power that made me say, "Well... I get upset if I do not succeed in doing what I aim for, and realize that it is *my* fault, for not trying harder and doing all that I am capable of to succeed." It must have been the correct answer, or in any case one that sufficiently impressed them, and when the school year rolled around, I was amongst the 90 out of 950 applicants who started their academic journey in psychology. That sentence, that I so nonchalantly relayed to 'them', actually defines me. It takes me time, checking, assessing, consulting and thinking, but, as the title of this part implies, once I decide on a goal, my motivation, actions, and behaviors are geared in a laser-like fashion to achieving it. This is not without struggle, for that is impossible, and if the journey was easy or uncomplicated, it would require no commitment or resolve.

 I am reminded of an experience that Wayne Dyer, the American psychologist, once relayed in a presentation he gave. He was committed to good health and as such took up jogging, which he did once even on a plane, as it was a long flight and he was not prepared to forego his exercise. But the truly amazing story that he told was of a marathon in which he participated. After four and a half hours of running, he was sitting/lying down exhausted and possibly vomiting. As he lay there, a TV reporter recognized him and asked him about his run, and Dyer exclaimed, "Yeah! I ran and I won!" The reporter looked at him inquisitively and replied, "Mr. So-and-so [I forget this character in the story's name] came in first at two hours and 19 minutes, and by now, he is probably on his way home." To which Dyer replied, "Well, yes – anyone can run for two hours and quit. I ran for four and a half hours, broke my record and won!"

I learned an important lesson from that story: I win whenever I give it my all, manage to break my own record, and arrive at my goal, regardless of how many arrived there with me, or before me.

> Some of the world's greatest feats were accomplished by
> people not smart enough to know they were impossible.
>
> Doug Larson

PSYCHOLOGY: CHOOSING WITH THE HEART

Apparently, choice is freedom. It is freeing to be able to choose, but it also means that *we*, the choosers, must assume responsibility for the results of that choice. I frequently hear parents and youngsters reflecting on their path in life and what they want to do. Truth be told, I did not have much to consider. It was a burning in my gut, a yearning of my soul, a very strong desire to become a psychologist and I was determined to do it. Too often I hear young people asking whether the field of their choice will bring them a *lot* of money. I do not hear, "Can I live on it?", but rather a query about getting a hefty income.

As someone who now looks back at 45 years in psychology (starting with my undergraduate studies) since I jumped over the entrance obstacles, I can see that it is the heart, not the money, the soul and not the riches, which must rule. If the most important factor in choosing a career is its ability to make you wealthy, then I am not sure that university is for you, and suspect that psychology is clearly not. True, computer studies and such may later allow you to hit the market with a startup that will bring you a fortune, but the number of hugely successful startups, in terms of percentages, is incredibly small. If you choose to study something that you are not totally convinced you are interested in, there is a good chance that you will either choose a field for which you have no aptitude, or one that does not 'turn you on', and thus, in both cases, you are doomed. If the chosen field does not suit you, you will either not be able to do well (having no aptitude) or you will risk low motivation and possibly drop out, for we usually persevere and do well in an area that we are interested in, and usually we are interested in areas in which we do well. So, should you altogether disregard the potential of your studies to make you wealthy? No, not when there are two areas that you are truly and equally interested in – then it makes sense to choose the one that promises a better life. But otherwise, go with your heart, unless you have a crystal ball and can read the distant future. For who knows what you will end up doing? Lawyers go into politics, David Cameron, the prime minister of Great Britain, came from marketing, and people with various degrees in any number of fields end up as administrators. So in the beginning of your academic journey, you actually have no idea what will happen a decade or 15 years hence – all the more reason to let the heart rule and get into what you really like.

Chapter 2

CHOOSING A UNIVERSITY AND GETTING IN

Discipline is the bridge between goals and accomplishment.
Jim Rohn

It was ten minutes to midnight, and the PR system at the York University library announced that we must leave, as the place was about to close. I was startled, having been so involved in the task at hand that I must have entered an altered state of consciousness, where the world around me actually 'ceased to exist', and I ignored inner and outer stimuli. It had been five hours since I had started. I did not hear those around me, nor did I feel hunger. Even my washroom breaks were few and very short.

What was I doing so intently? It was 1973, shortly after I had arrived in Canada. I had a B.A. in Psychology and another one in Philosophy from Tel Aviv University, and was attempting to gain entry into graduate school. From Israel I had applied to York University's clinical psychology program, but not being fluent in English, not realizing how extremely competitive the clinical psychology track is, and being completely ignorant of the 'politics' that play a pivotal role in the academic journey, I did not have a chance.

I think that it was Nietzsche who so profoundly observed that we must live our lives forwards, but can only understand them backwards, and so, while I was heartbroken at the time for not getting into the graduate program at York, years later, I was thankful for it, for a variety of reasons that are not pertinent to our present discussion. Upon arriving in Canada, and after being shunned by York, I started to acquaint myself with other universities and programs. Each had a long list of requirements, and I became more and more disheartened. Not for a minute did my fire stop burning and I knew that I would still study psychology, but I was quite clueless as to where to begin and how to go about it.

This book is written precisely because there are so many people in similar situations, and there is nowhere to turn. I know it from my undergraduate students, who reflect on their confusion at graduating from high school, and four years later, when they wish to continue their studies and get advanced degrees, they, like me, do not know how to do it.

Back to the library: I realized that reading and examining universities' minimum entrance expectations would not get me anywhere. It is similar to misleading advertising that claim to sell cars, houses or vacation from X amount of dollars. It is knowing what you get at each price range and what you will end up paying that is important. This is probably the only important fact. So, in those pre-computer and internet days, I sat in the university's library with a huge American Psychological Association (APA)-published book, which reviewed all of the APA-approved psychology programs in North America and provided me with 'golden' information that really shed some light on the dark alley I was going through. It indicated the percentage of applicants who got accepted into each program – thus letting me zero in on those programs where I would have the best chance of being accepted – and described the characteristics of the lucky ones who were invited to study at those institutions. Now, when I had the *end* information, rather than the minimum entrance requirements, I was able to get a good sense of where I stood in comparison to those accepted, and whether I had a chance to get into a graduate program. I am certain that all of this information is also available to those seeking entrance to undergraduate programs.

But we are still not there, not yet ready to apply to a university. If you are like me, then distance from home or getting into the least expensive place are not really important. The most important ingredient, for me at least, was to get accepted into a good program. I often hear people – usually those who have a crystal ball – 'calculating' where it is best to attend, or commiserating that they are going 'nowhere' apart from the local universities, or attending the academic institutions that will end up getting them a higher-paying job. While some people will not relocate for various reasons (among them financial ones), there are others who wish to attend the same university that their parents attended. But, in general, I suggest that you go to the best academic institution that your grades and letters of reference can get you into, and for which you can afford to pay. I never decided *a priori* where I would attend, and thus I applied in my town, my province, and all over North America. All I wanted was to get in, study psychology, and get closer to the next (higher) degree. Naturally, when I did have a choice, my choice was based on a variety of personal and situational factors, but one thing alone guided me: I wanted to attend a university that would best prepare me for the next rung in the academic ladder. Unless, of course, as happened when I applied for the Masters degree, I was accepted into only one university and so that is where I went, but we will address that later.

I realize that some of the decisions about where to study may rely on parental influence (especially if they are paying or helping to pay for it), whether you need to remain near your employment if you must work, or whether your boy/girlfriend can or cannot move with you. These last issues are unique to each individual and no-one can tell you what and how to take these into account. They are influenced by cultural, financial, and romantic factors, which play a part in all our lives, and no-one but you can decide how to handle them.

> When it is obvious that the goals cannot be reached,
> don't adjust the goals, adjust the action steps.
>
> Confucius

Chapter 3

ATTENDING UNDERGRADUATE SCHOOL

People who say it cannot be done should not interrupt those who are doing it.
George Bernard Shaw

It was my first university class in the fall of 1969. I felt exhilarated after two failed attempts to get accepted into a very demanding psychology undergraduate program, one among only three such programs in Israel at the time, but I was also highly anxious. It reminded me of the time just before my wedding night. This was, essentially, entering a path that was unknown to me. I looked around and there were many psychologists in the media and on the psychological register. But I wondered whether they were smart, talented, capable, and had what it takes to graduate and become what I was yearning to be – a graduate of a psychology program and eventually a psychologist. I was highly doubtful then that I had all of those coveted characteristics.

Prof. Leibowitz, a well-known psychologist, philosopher, and chemist, was the first 'sample' of professors that I encountered. There were about 90 of us in the class. Some people knew each other and were talking in a hushed tone, while the rest of us newbies were staring at the professor, trying with all our might to follow him, but to no avail. Being a good teacher, as I learned over the years, is not just *knowing* the material, but knowing *how* to present it, and, just as important, being wise enough to follow the students and their reactions. Prof. Leibowitz, a brilliant scientist and thinker, was hovering about seven atmospheric levels above us, not realizing that we had just started our academic journey and had almost no idea what he was talking about. The other students did not act in the disheartened way that I was intensely feeling. I remember that first year of university was difficult for me. First and foremost, I 'lost' my identity and very quickly became a faceless body in a sea of students, seated in large halls, listening to professors who had no idea who we were, or whether we were even able to follow and understand them. In academia, you will find some professors – some young and some less so, men and women, and some quite attractive – which prove to be hazardous to one's concentration. There were those who spoke to and even with the students, those who read the material that they had summarized in their notebook, and those who spoke as if they had just graduated from a course for radio announcers, and thus spoke in a loud voice and crisp sentences, while others murmured such that it was almost impossible to understand them. And then was the course material, which could be quite challenging.

A week before university started, the group of 90 newbies were invited to a meeting with the chairman of the department. We were all very excited since the majority of us harbored dreams of becoming clinical psychologists, imagining ourselves seeing clients in our offices, and offering calming 'herbs' for their tortured souls via therapy. The chairman must have known about our hidden dreams, or may have had the exact same ones when he was our age. He welcomed us and congratulated the 90 excited future students that outperformed the other 900 who had not been accepted. He then proceeded to describe to us the 'excitement' that awaits us. "There are two main things that I want you to take away from this meeting," he said:

1. "Although you may have envisioned 'curing' patients, during the next three years, you ain't gonna see any patients at all, until you enter graduate school. That is simply because you would not know what to do with them; additionally,
2. "Excitement, treatment methods, and in-depth knowledge of psychological assessment and disturbances will all be found if and when you enter graduate school. For the next three years, all you will do is become acquainted with the history of psychology; learn what was done, developed and theorized in the past 100 years. And," he added, "that may not always be interesting, empowering or what you were hoping for, but this is the foundation of psychology, which you must be familiar with before you go on."

I felt as if the air was drained out of my lungs. It was not going to be what I dreamed of after all. But – and this was something that I reminded myself throughout my academic journey and helped me get through it – I am part of a system that has the authority and the power to grant me a degree, and a very small par at that, so that when I go out into the real world, I can do what I like and what 'turns me on'.

The first year was a challenge, for not only was I a part of a 'machinery' that was unfamiliar to me, I was also unsure of how to handle a school that did not pile mountains of homework on me and was unclear on how to motivate myself to keep up with the readings when no teacher checked on me (as was the case in elementary and high schools) and how to prepare for exams. Exams forever increased my blood pressure and anxiety, and aroused doubts about my suitability for university education. I quickly discovered that I performed much better when we were asked to write a final paper in a course, but mostly had to answer multiple-choice exams, for which I was not 'wired' to excel. I finished my first undergraduate year with several observations and insights:

a. While I was an average student, I did pass all the courses, and even if I had not, I knew that I would find a way to retake those tests in a different date and succeed. I *knew* – I did not just feel but *knew* – that I would do all the studying that I needed to do, and succeed.

b. Once I passed the first year, I took it as 'proof' that I could indeed handle university, and as such, I would see it to the end of undergraduate school.

c. I learned that I may not have had much confidence in my abilities, but once I was convinced that I can handle the task at hand, I would go on to the finish line. Despite trials, tribulations, and obstacles, quitting was not what I did. This perseverance, going on despite doubts and obstacles, and sometimes even setbacks, is what got me to where I am today.

d. When I encountered rough terrain on my way to obtaining a B.A., I sought help from anyone who was ready and able to offer it: the professors, their teaching assistants, or my classmates. I readily admitted to not knowing or understanding something, and found that, regardless of the subject I had difficulty with, someone was there to make my ride smoother and my understanding clearer.

e. In first year, I looked up from the first rung on which I stood at second- and third-year students with awe and admiration, for they were the ones who had mastered the first year and progressed to where I was heading. Seeing them in the university's hallways and by unobtrusively listening to their talks, I realized that some were truly smart and even gifted, but the rest were just average students like me, and that observation stood me in good stead when I encountered bumps in the undergraduate road. If they could do it, I said to myself, then so could I, and I continued to progress, despite occasional stormy seas.

Earlier, I mentioned my wedding night. I got married a week before starting university and, as such, it was clear to me that I would study psychology, but since the academic schedule is commonly checkered – a class here and several free hours there – I would also work and contribute to the household economy. Therefore, I worked during the days or blocks of time where I had no classes. Truth be told, I was very busy. But I felt a sense of accomplishment since I was going to school, performing well academically, and additionally succeeding in the world of work. Upon reaching the end of undergraduate school, I reflected on the lessons I had learned, which I will address in the next chapter.

> Universities are full of knowledge; the freshmen bring a little in and the seniors take none away, and knowledge accumulates.
> Abbott L. Lowell

Chapter 4

LESSONS I LEARNED IN UNDERGRADUATE SCHOOL

> Never tell me the sky's the limit when there are footprints on the moon.
> Unknown author

Getting into university is like looking for employment – it's a full-time job. While we proceed from elementary to high school directly and usually with little input into the process, the change from high school to university is a major one. Previously, I addressed some of the questions we must ask ourselves prior to choosing which university to attend, but additionally, once we zero in on the one or two universities that we are interested in and hope to attend, it is a good idea – if it is practical – to visit the campus, find out who is on the committee that chooses next year's students, and meet with that person or people for a chat, leaving with them your curriculum vitae (CV) and a good impression of you. It also makes good sense to speak with first- and second-year university students and inquire about their academic experience (to verify that you still wish to attend that academic institution), about housing, and about social life.

Another important, although by no means crucial factor is to check whether the institution of your choice offers a graduate degree in the program of your choice, and how difficult it is to get into their graduate-level program.

While attending university, you invariably look around, assess your peers in and out of your program, and zero in on those who are seemingly blessed by inner beauty, striking features, and the ones who seem 'smart', bright, and capable of getting good grades effortlessly. At least, that has been my experience. We need to remember that it is natural to assess and even compare yourself to your peers. As you do so, you will notice that there are those who look physically better or worse than you, those who are more or less socially successful than you, and those who may be doing better, much better, or worse than you academically. That is a given of university life. The question that *is* important is how it affects you. If you can accept that the university population is representative of the population at large in looks and intelligence, then you know that there are people who are more or less blessed than you are in various 'departments'. But if this will negatively affect your self-esteem – if 'their' academic success indicates to you that you may not be cut out for academic education – then you have got a problem. I recall that I was, indeed, intimidated by others' successes, and consequently doubted my own abilities. However, I did not let that affect my goal, path, or end point. I continued to do my best by repeatedly telling myself that as long as I did not fail courses, I would soldier on, regardless of my worries about my intellectual potential. While I realized that I may not be the brightest and sharpest pencil in the box, I held this thought separately from my motivation and conviction that I would complete the path I had chosen, and apparently, this paid off.

Assignments and Writing Papers

When he was in the second year of his undergraduate psychology program, my son once came to me to ask which topic he should write a paper about. The professor had asked the class to pick a topic from a list and write about it. So he did what most students tend to do – he chose a topic that interested him, and then roamed the university library in search for relevant books upon which he could base his paper. He had found some relevant books, but they were not really helpful.

I shared with him the principle that guided me in university in general, but in undergraduate school in particular – my interest came second to completing assignments and getting good grades. So when I would get such an assignment where I had to 'pick' a topic, I spent several hours on books that were related to the subject of the course, with the list of assigned topics in my hand, leafing through books, reading the tables of contents, and examining whether I could understand the book, and whether its 'scaffolding' – as presented in the table of contents – was such that it could be integrated into my paper with relative ease. What I was searching for was not a topic of interest to write about, but one where the available resources would make it as good as I could write it, thus resulting in a high grade. This approach proved itself useful and served me well throughout my academic journey.

MORE AND LESS INTERESTING COURSES

Most undergraduate courses are required: you must take them. You are sometimes allowed to choose the section to study, and if so, lucky you! In that case, check who the professor is, whether his past exams were difficult or 'manageable', and what previous students think of the course. In light of all that, decide which section you will join. As for elective courses, pick and choose those that interest you, but mainly check out your chances to do well in them. Not all courses will be easy, interesting, or seem useful, but you must enroll in them to graduate. Identify your strengths and weaknesses (my strengths were writing papers and not exams, and statistics was really challenging for me), and get assistance in those areas or subjects where there is room for improvement. The goal is to do well, and so do whatever you can to improve your skills so that you get better grades. Leave your ego at the door! It is better to seek and get help than to avoid acknowledging that you need it – and fail.

PROFESSORS

Professors are the university's foundation. They have at their disposal the knowledge that you seek and the grades that you are after. In the first year of your undergraduate program, while sitting in a hall holding hundreds of first-year students, all you may see is a distant figure, speaking through a microphone, not recognizing any students, and being aided by a small 'army' of teaching assistants who also do not know you and, should they be responsible for many students, may not even remember you. But once first year is behind you, then you need to start to think, plan, and act to increase your chances of being accepted into graduate school.

Therefore, the end of your first year is the time to visit your 'favorite' professors in their offices, present yourself, and offer to volunteer to assist in their research. If accepted – and I suggest that you offer to help more than just one professor – you win twice: you will learn about research, data collection, literature review, and more, and if you do a really good job for the professor and assist him for a sufficient length of time so that they can get to know you, you will most likely get a good letter of reference, or even get chosen by that very same professor to enroll in graduate school, should you apply. I, for instance, reward my good and long-serving volunteer research assistants by enrolling them in a conference that deals with the research that they contributed to, and they go and present a paper there.

LEARNING, PERFORMING, ENJOYING

I presume that in this day and age, when you need something from the university library, you click your mouse and find it. Then, you either download the article, or read the book's table of contents, unless you find an e-book and download the whole thing. In my pre-internet days, we walked amongst the book stacks. I love reading and spent my childhood and adolescent years devouring books. I would walk amongst the shelves that were stacked with hundreds of thousands of books, and as I was searching for the book or books for my courses, assignments, or tests, I would come by various exciting discoveries: books that were interesting, engaging, and aroused my curiosity. I would quickly leaf through them and, with a heavy heart, put them back, sometimes writing their title and call number for a future time when I would be able to read them. Studying psychology, working, and preparing for classes and exams left little time for anything else. As much as it was tempting to take the time and read a book that my heart desired, I knew that it would take away from the limited time that I had to do school work, and I was not prepared to sacrifice any future grades for a book – as wonderful as it may be. So, I ended up reading, thinking, and dealing with psychology most of my waking hours, but did so only with the material that I was expected to study and on which I would later be tested.

As previously noted, reaching my goal (and for you, your own goal) is what was and is of prime importance, and if you have enrolled in psychology studies, it should not be so that you can sample it (via enrolling in an undergraduate degree), but rather you should intend to go all the way.

Chapter 5

APPLYING AND GETTING INTO GRADUATE SCHOOL

A musician must make music, an artist must paint, a poet must write, if he is to be ultimately at peace with himself.
What a man can be, he must be.

Abraham Maslow

Getting into graduate school is the dream of everyone who wants to become a psychologist. It is the major goal that will then pave the way towards getting into the profession of psychology. Consequently, applying to graduate school has to be planned, researched, and intentionally executed.

As I described my case some 35 years ago, it may serve you well if you check which universities offer the program that you wish to attend, and from amongst these, zero in on those departments who accept the highest percentage of applicants for the program that you are interested in, and those where your characteristics and strengths approximate those of students who were accepted. Your CV is your business card. It is supposed to 'sell' you to the professors of that university. So ensure that it is complete, accurate, and presented in a manner that will entice those professors and make them want to pick *you* from amongst all the rest. I doubt that there is only one way of preparing a CV, but there is clearly one goal – do it in such a way that, while honest and humble, it will present you in the best possible light and in a manner that will draw attention to your strengths and achievements.

As a practicing clinician and a university professor, I speak with my third- or fourth-year students about the need to have research experience, which they can get through volunteering with a professor, ending up with a sparkling letter of reference. I feel sad when I receive an email asking for a reference about six to 12 months after a course that I taught is over. I always have doubts whether that student who wrote to me, knowing that I do not really know them, will succeed in getting into a graduate program, being so unprepared and unable to do what is required in order to get known by professors, and so get good letters of reference. In general, I will comply with the request and write a letter, unless I cannot find anything good to say about that person. However, I feel ethically bound (and the recommendation form frequently inquires as to the length of time I have known the student) to elucidate that we had only minimal interaction for a short period of time. A letter like that does not carry much weight.

When I applied to graduate programs, I did not know all of what was involved, and no-one was there to guide me or give me inside information. In my applications to clinical graduate programs, I wrote that I wanted to enter the clinical graduate programs because, "I wanted to help people and ease their pain," which is what I am doing to this day. But at that time, the entrance committees must have chuckled and passed me over in favor of other candidates. I believe that if you have an interesting CV, good undergraduate grades, have been a research assistant, and possess heartwarming (the hearts of the professors you want to impress, that is) letters of reference, you may have a good chance of success. Being 'fluent' in statistical analysis and having some provisional research interests that may be interesting to one or more of the professors who are teaching at the desired departments could seal the deal.

When I applied to graduate school and was told that I had been placed on a waiting list, I found out who the chair of the admissions committee was and spoke with her on several occasions. There is a possibility that she let me into the program just to get me off her back, but nonetheless, I succeeded in getting into a graduate program. It was not my first choice, not an Ivy League university, and not located in the city where I resided. But such minor imperfections did not mean much to me. I knew that a Master's degree would get me closer to a Ph.D. degree, and that brought the 'working world' – with me as a psychologist who could actually earn some money – within reach.

I was delighted to be accepted into that program and trusted that I could complete graduate school. I celebrated, made arrangements to move into residence (two guys in a small room, with the showers, toilet, and kitchenette at the end of the corridor), and, when the day came to leave my home and travel to the university, my excitement could hardly been any more intense.

Chapter 6

GRADUATE SCHOOL

> Education is one of the chief obstacles to intelligence and freedom of thought.
>
> Bertrand Russell

It felt so good to be walking the hallways of the psychology department on the first day of my graduate (M.A.) studies. I was excited, full of anticipation, anxious, wondering how I would do, and sorely missing my family, who resided about 90 minutes away by car.

After years of undergraduate study in which I attended huge classes, it amazed me to be in a class of 20 students, and to see that the professor remembered my name. I felt both exhilarated for being in graduate school but also tense and very alert in order to ensure that I would realize all of those hopes that were pinned on me by my family and the educational institution. The first semester passed very quickly, with me getting to know the professors and my classmates, attempting to master the material, being fortunate to land a research assistantship job with one of the professors, going home (four hours by bus) on weekends, and preparing for the end-of-semester exams. A week before the end of the semester, I felt quite sick, and was very weak. The university physician who examined me smiled and informed me that it must be stress-related, offering to back me up should I wish to postpone exams – I declined.

Over the years, I had been frequently visited by excessive stress. I realized that despite the pressing need that I felt to study and keep up, I needed to balance studying, tension, anxiety, and responsibility with time off, relaxation, a lighter load, and physical activity. Realizing this, and after several unsuccessful trials, putting this into effect helped my body regenerate, my spirits soar, my muscles relax, and my social life (which was almost non-existent during the full-throttle academic study) flourished.

Two particularly poignant experiences from my graduate studies towards my M.A. degree are still with me. One includes the time that I wrote a critical analysis of a book published by the well-known theorist Chris Argyris, a writer who my course director adored. All I wanted was a good grade. However, in addition to the A+ that I received, the paper also bore a note whereby my professor asked my permission to add parts of my "excellent and insightful paper" to his own feedback, which he planned to send to Argyris. The second incident that I vividly remember occurred in another seminar. The students were asked to write a paper, and on the due date, when we brought our papers to the class to hand in to the professor, he instructed us to exchange our papers and read and grade each other's work. Upon getting back my paper, I saw a grade of 'B' had been given to me by whoever had read it. The professor then took home all the papers and read and graded them himself – mine was changed to an 'A'.

Why do I share those two experiences?

a. To highlight the fact that our peers (be they students or full-fledged professionals) tend to judge us very harshly, hence the existence of 'peer-reviewed journals', and we may consequently and unnecessarily adopt their criticism as a true reflection of our abilities or of who we are; and

b. During my Masters degree years, I was plagued by questions pertaining to my ability to graduate. I 'collected' and cherished each indication that came my way that I was on the right track and had what it takes, and I seemed to get somewhat frequent approval from those I looked up to – my professors.

Prior to graduation from the M.A. degree, I added to my already full workload with the search, inquiry, assessment, and application preparation for Ph.D. programs. While I was finishing my thesis, preparing to defend it, and ensuring that all was taken care of, including working and earning money, I had an experience the likes of which I had never previously had. All three universities to which I had applied accepted me to their Ph.D. programs, and after much deliberation and checking the pros and cons of each, I chose to attend the university that I understood was the best of the three. It was Purdue University in the Midwest of the USA. I had to leave my family, and for the next 20 months, lived in university residence, which was a very simple building, with a very small room bereft of a bathroom, toilet, or kitchen, but within my financial means and, most importantly, right on campus. That last fact was an important one, as it enabled me to get to classes regardless of traffic or weather conditions, and if I had a large 'window' of time in between classes, I could go to my room and study, eat (and so avoid the much less healthy food on campus), or have a short nap, which would then enable me to study into the late night hours.

Since my family remained in Toronto, I was determined to complete my Ph.D. studies as fast as I could. School commenced on September 4th and although it took a while to get acquainted with the geography of the campus, meet the professors, start the courses that I was required to enroll in, and meet some of my classmates, I also worked on preparing a dissertation proposal complete with an extensive literature review, and planned the relevant statistical analyses. In November of that year, after several reminders, I received the verdict from my supervising faculty who read my proposal, which was 'topic not suitable'. This was partly a result of my choosing an esoteric subject that my supervising faculty did not like. It would take me some time to realize that, while in university, my goal would not be to research what peaked my own interest, but what would help me pass and progress into real life.

In January of the following year (i.e., two months later), I submitted a new dissertation proposal that, after a long and tension-filled six-week wait, came back with the same disheartening message, bringing me back to square one for the third time. Three months later – and after an irate supervisor inquired as to why was I in such a rush (he believed that good guys finish last) and why I could not simply do "what everyone else does," meaning complete the courses and only then compile a dissertation proposal – I was given the go-ahead.

The courses I enrolled in were interesting, the treatment of us – the Ph.D. cohort – was reasonable, and the easy access we had to the faculty underscored the understanding that the university as an organization would treat us as those who will soon – whenever that may have been – join the ranks of those with a Ph.D. degree. All of this contributed to the Ph.D. experience being, for me, the best, easiest, and most pleasant of the three degree programs that I undertook over the years. I worked on my dissertation – which focused on cooperative versus competitive behaviors – as I was preparing for the dreaded 'prelims' (the counterpart of the Canadian 'comps' or comprehensive examinations). It took four months of studying almost around the clock to prepare for that four-day long, eight hours per day exam, which tested us on all the material that we had learned in the Ph.D. program. Describing that exam as grueling is an understatement. Seeing a classmate who was the 'favorite' of the department's faculty, the apple of their eye, and the one who was predicted to get a university position immediately upon graduation (since he was considered so bright and capable) fail that exam and endure untold humiliation strengthened my resolve to be well prepared for it – and so I was, and passed it successfully. That was the toughest hurdle of my academic journey and it was now behind me. I just needed to finish my dissertation and defend it – and then I would be done.

My supervising faculty member was not one to complete tasks on time and I needed to be armed with a lot of patience, perseverance, and diplomacy in order to get him to finish reading and evaluating my dissertation, which was revised within a week and offered to him again, much to his chagrin. I am convinced that he let out a big sigh of relief when I graduated.

I was sweaty and anxious upon entering the 'defense room', meeting three faculty members who were about to 'grill' me on my dissertation. It took an hour of time and lots of brainpower to help them see that I knew what I was doing in my research/dissertation. At the end, I was told to leave the room, knowing full well that, until they completed their critique of my performance and I returned to meet them, I would not know whether I had passed (and thus fulfilled all of my requirements) or failed.

My favorite committee member came out to invite me back in, after 15 nerve-grating minutes, and while he was prohibited from telling me whether I had passed or failed, he creatively invited me to come back in by saying, "Dr. Rokach, the committee is waiting for you." How sweet those words were as a culmination of eight arduous years, Herculean efforts, and not taking my eyes off the target for a moment! Two weeks later, after applying some required minor corrections to the dissertation, and wishing goodbye to my Bell Boy peers in the campus hotel in which I had worked for two years, I was on the plane heading back to Toronto, still unable to believe that I had reached the summit and completed the task that I had undertaken eight years earlier.

Chapter 7

LIFE AFTER THE DEGREE

Be who you are and say what you feel, because those who mind don't matter and those who matter don't mind.

Dr. Seuss

When I returned to Toronto, I did not have much time to enjoy the 'freedom' from school that I achieved by finishing my Ph.D. Competition to land a position in my field was stiff and consequently, I quickly realized that simply applying for a job and waiting for a positive reply was not going to get me anywhere. I started to plan to upgrade my skills, in order to enhance my chances of finding employment. I did so on two fronts: academically and professionally. I joined the graduate program at a local university and, over the course of a year, completed four courses that I felt could help upgrade my skills. It was a joy to attend university and enroll in courses without worrying about the grades that I would receive or whether it would help me gain entrance to the next phase of my academic journey. I studied because I wanted to, enrolled in courses that interested me, and although I was writing exams and papers, I 'aced it', and it was sheer fun to do these courses regardless of the grade that awaited me at the end of the semester.

I wanted to join the College of Psychology, the governing body of psychologists, and prepared for the demanding exams and interview that I had to pass. I needed to find a supervisor who, after a full year, could attest to my preparedness to act as a clinical psychologist and independently offer psychotherapy. For about 15 months, I was supervised by a very experienced psychologist in an outpatient clinic that treated sufferers of anxiety conditions, phobias, and depression. I joined that clinic as a volunteer, and after getting to know me for a while, the psychologist agreed to supervise me for the college's purpose. I discovered that psychology – and possibly other fields as well – is like driving. You take a driving course (i.e., complete your education) so that you could get a license and be qualified to drive (i.e., practice). But you really learn to drive once you are on the road handling the car by yourself. It is once you obtain supervision and see clients that you learn how to really offer therapy, psychological assessment, and instigate the sprouting of the kernel that will become your clinical acumen.

My supervisor taught me so much that it whet my appetite. After about the first six months in that clinic, I requested – and was granted – a meeting with the chief psychologist in another psychiatric hospital. The reason that I applied for a second postdoctoral position was that I was bent on learning whatever I could on couple and sex therapy, which was taught there and I intended to later practice. I met with the chief psychologist, showed him my CV, and did my best to impress him, and he accepted me for postdoctoral training in psychodynamic psychotherapy. I inquired about the sex therapy clinic that his institution had and he told me that the application period for a postdoctoral position there was over, and that they had accepted all the people that they could handle, and thus I had to stay in his program of psychodynamic psychotherapy. That was not what I wanted. I inquired as to the name of the head of the sex therapy clinic. The chief psychologist gave it to me reluctantly. I called and the head of the sex therapy program then invited me for an interview. She was one of the most intelligent, graceful, and pleasant professionals that I have ever met. We 'clicked' immediately, and she explained to me that the chief psychologist, being a Freudian, did not think much of her sex therapy clinic, which helped me understand why he tried to steer me away from meeting with her. She was glad for me to join and I had one of my best, most enjoyable, and enriching 18 months professionally. This taught me once again that a 'No' is but a wall or obstacle that is put on one's path in order to check how creative one is in scaling it, going around it, below it, or beside it!

My son, Ben, is now 30 years old and in the last stage of his residency and training to become a radiologist. Like all parents, I sought to serve as his model in life and did so in two ways: by talking with him about what is important and worth 'fighting' for; and through my behavior, which is the most convincing way to influence someone. During his years in elementary school, high school and university, I repeatedly spoke with him about setting a goal – once he knew what he wanted to achieve – and not veering from it, going on despite obstacles and in the face of whatever boulders and sandstorms that may block his path.

It seems that Ben internalized the message, and pushed on when I was ready to give up. For more than a decade, I have been teaching a full year of introduction to counseling to small classes of 20 to 25 fourth-year students. We covered the theories and the 'nuts and bolts' of helping clients. Being such a small class, we created a pleasant, interesting, and almost intimate atmosphere where learning occurred in a fun and creative manner.

When Ben was planning his fourth-year schedule, aiming to get a B.Sc. in psychology so that he could later apply to medical school (which he did and has now completed), he approached me one day with a unique request: "I heard from my friends, who enrolled in your course last year, how much fun it was and I plan to be your student in the coming year!" I was touched that my son wanted to enroll in the course that I taught. I thought it could be really neat to have him see another part of my life, and compare my being a father to being his university professor. I looked at him and, sadly, said: "You know that it is against the rules, and being my son you will not be allowed to enroll in my class." He was quiet and pensive.

The following day, Ben told me that he spoke with Ann, the department executive secretary, and she suggested that he speak with the Dean. He was encouraged that she had not shot down his idea, instead indicating that the Dean may, under some conditions, approve it. Ben met with the Dean the following week and returned home with a huge smile plastered on his face. "How come," he teased me, "you gave up, after teaching me to not do what you just did? So knowing that giving up is not an option, I met with the Dean and he approved my attendance in your class, provided that another faculty grades me." I was truly delighted, not only that Ben would join my class, but also that he had internalized my message and had not given up. I was simply anxious, wondering whether my class may not be all that receptive to my son being amongst them, and that his friends' prior experience in my class would not repeat itself. That would be a shame – to have my son attend my class and not enjoy himself.

We were fortunate to be able to enlist another faculty member who graded his two exams: his in-class group presentation and his final paper. To my great joy, this was probably my best class ever. In our last meeting before the final exam, during a 'party' that we had (as I have in almost all my classes), I heard two of his classmates approach Ben, and not realizing that I could hear them, they said to him, "You are so lucky to have a father like the one who taught us." All's well that ends well. The class was a resounding success, and Ben achieved an A+ (as he did in the other five courses he took that year), and our shared in-class experience strengthened our already strong bond, deepening the affection and love that we felt for one another.

While Ben's academic journey was smoother than mine, he encountered similar debris, obstacles, and difficulties on his path. I cheered him on when he refused to budge, until he arrived 'on shore' safely. There is one additional point that needs to be explicitly stated. After you have invested enough time and resources in initially assessing whether your goal is reachable and meets your needs and desires, perseverance and not giving up on your goal are essential.

Chapter 8

BECOMING A CLINICAL PSYCHOLOGIST

> It always seems impossible until it's done.
>
> Nelson Mandela

I registered with the College of Psychologists, passed the exam and interview, and became a registered psychologist in the province of Ontario, Canada. I was now certified and allowed to present myself as a psychologist and treat people on my own, or 'independently', as the college put it. It was time to look back and assess what had helped me achieve the designation of a clinical psychologist, and plan where to go from there.

As I started my 'walk' in real life, taking one step at a time, I quickly realized that:

a. Just because I held a Ph.D. and a designation of a psychologist, this did not mean that I knew what I was doing. In other words, I did not feel at all ready to treat people, and thus I enrolled in the two postdoctoral training programs that I mentioned earlier.

b. I wanted to get some experience teaching, as I had absolutely no experience in this area. Many students work as teaching assistants during their graduate studies, but I avoided it since I was unsure whether I was cut out to stand before a group of people and talk – anxiety, you may call it.

c. I needed to look for a job, a real, full-time job, since I was not yet ready to start a private practice and also because I always knew that just 'doing' full-time private practice was not for me. I thought about what I liked in psychology, and concluded that, first and foremost, I liked to help people heal. But then, I was not ready to forego teaching and research, and so I decided to do all three.

Until I could find employment, and as I had a family by that time, I endeavored to look for any job I could get, and landed one as a van driver, delivering newspaper bundles at night to the kids who would then deliver them to their customers in the morning hours. I worked for the newspaper delivery department three nights a week, and did so for several months, giving it up only after I started working full-time as a psychologist, and was certain that I would remain employed in this role for the foreseeable future. I had no problem being probably the most highly educated deliveryman in Toronto, one with a Ph.D. in psychology. I enjoyed working at night, not having to do intellectual work during my shift, and knowing that I was done with my education, and that eventually I would find employment as a clinical psychologist.

Such an employment opportunity practically knocked on my door. One of my postdoctoral supervisors recommended that I attend a local psychology conference and seek out a Dr. Reg, the chief psychologist of a jail just outside of Toronto, who was looking for 'good people' to hire for his department. "A jail? Do I want to work in a jail, walking around with heavy keys all day surrounded by dangerous and hostile criminals?" I thought to myself as I headed to the conference to meet with Dr. Reg. He was pleasant and seemed kind, and before I applied for the position, he suggested that I visit the jail. I did so the following week and still remember my shock at realizing that my preconceived ideas about jails, mean-looking jailers, and movie-fed pictures of rows of cages fell by the wayside, one by one. It was the opposite of the menacing place that I had expected to find, and after meeting informally with several department members, I applied for the position and was accepted after an interview. I remained there longer than a Canadian 'life sentence', which stands at 25 years. I retired from there after 28 years, having fully enjoyed (almost) every minute of working there! I will talk more about the jail and what I learned there later.

A well-known community college was situated about five minutes' drive from the jail. I arranged a meeting with the director of continuing education at this college, and I met with him one day during my lunch break. Following a short meeting in which I was successful at demonstrating to him that I had the knowledge and ability (I had the knowledge but lied about my ability) to teach his mature evening students, he said, "I have all the courses that I need taught, with assigned instructors to them. Develop a course and I will let you teach it." So began my teaching experience that has lasted 35 years and counting. I met the director again the following month and showed him the outline of a course entitled 'Psychology in everyday life', and got the go-ahead to teach it in the following semester. Many different courses – which I did not need to develop but were already listed in the calendar – followed, and six years later, I was accepted as a contract faculty at a local university – York University – where I still teach to this day. Again, I did not just apply for a position at the community college, but worked to make it happen. Once I opened the door, other things at that college and beyond came my way.

Within the first year of working in the jail – or the 'correctional institution', as it is referred to – I was already searching for a subfield in psychology in which I could do my research and contribute to the knowledge that the scientific community is forever producing and consuming. My search was successful after I attended a psychology conference in 1981 and found myself realizing that what I wanted to study was loneliness. My peers, in the jail and beyond, were surprised that I had chosen such an esoteric and unpopular subject (as it was in 1981) for my research, sent 'digs' my way about possible 'personal, unresolved loneliness issues', and suggested other more popular topics on which I could focus. Once I had read some books and pivotal articles on loneliness, I became aware of the paucity of accumulated knowledge on this topic, and knew that, despite not being cheered on by my peer, this would be my chosen area.

SUPERVISION

I frequently remind my students that the best thing that they can do for their career is to find a good, or if possible an excellent supervisor. I got one, initially against my will. About a month after I started to work in the correctional institute, Dr. Reg, the chief psychologist, came into my office, sat down, and asked his eternal question: "What have you done for me today?" That would start a discussion about work and psychology-related issues. Then he said, "How would you feel if I invited you to meet with me weekly in my office and discuss psychology and how you practice it?" Shocked, but not willing to disagree with my new boss, I agreed. When he left my office, I remember saying to myself in horror, "Up until now, I doubted that I knew what I am doing – now he doubts it too." I was embarrassed, scared, and apprehensive. Reg and I started to meet and held weekly meetings where he supervised, guided and directed me and deeply influenced my thinking and understanding of psychology and what a clinical psychologist does. We ended those meetings after three years, reluctantly on my part, as Reg announced, "I've taught you all that I know." He was exaggerating. Twice before I succeeded in postponing the inevitable end of our weekly meetings, and now I relented. His supervision was such an eye-opener, horizon-widener and a learning lab that I have relied on his lessons repeatedly for the past 30 years. Reg also introduced me to the writings of the American psychiatrist Robert Langs, which left a strong impression on me. To this day, his writing continues to structure the ground rules and affects the trajectory of my approach to helping people.

Over the years, I have frequently thought to myself that, at the time that Reg suggested supervision to me, had I been terrified of being 'found out' and not had the courage to look at how I was practicing psychology (or, conversely, had I been cocky and arrogant, convincing myself that holding a Ph.D. meant that I knew all I need to know), I would have missed out on an exceptionally enriching period, both professionally and personally, and would have most probably not been introduced to Langs' writings and so would have missed the joy of continued professional growth.

WHAT I HAVE LEARNED IN SCHOOL AND IN SUPERVISION

At that point in my budding career, I was able to reflect on my school years and what I had learned during my postdoctoral training and first year of work, and make several observations:

a. Training to become a psychologist is a long and arduous track. Just to be accepted into graduate school is not easy, but as you advance from one degree to the next, the material is more interesting, and I found being taught how to attend and counsel clients to be exhilarating, and it remains so. The material that we were taught ranged from difficult and demanding (for me, statistics was one such subject) to interesting, easy, and enriching (which I found to be the case for abnormal psychology,

      counseling and psychotherapy, and personality and psychopathology).
b. The teaching faculty are as important as the material they teach. Some left an indelible mark on me and influenced me positively for years after I left school. Those were often not the 'smartest', most published professors, but the ones who showed an interest in students and listened to and supported them when they needed it.
c. It is important that we familiarize ourselves with theories and with all of the other professional areas that we are exposed to over the years. However, you may not be surprised to learn that while it is important to know such theories, this may not be especially helpful when you 'do' psychology.
d. Since all the knowledge that you are bombarded with during your school years is cumulative, what you were taught in your highest degree program will be the most remembered and of the most practical importance.
e. Practicum, which you are exposed to in seminars and workshops while at school, is likely to be very important and helpful to your future career. These provided me with the most concentrated, enlightening, and hands-on information and skills that I was later able to practice on my own.
f. Being exposed to books by specific writers – Freud, Rogers, Langs, and Yalom – was for me like walking into the Land of Oz, where I could partake in their adventures and insights. I later adopted some of their outlooks in my approach to the complex field of psychotherapy.
g. Upon graduation, I relatively quickly identified areas that I needed to learn more about and skills that I needed to acquire in order to enhance my chances of finding employment. I thus enrolled in the two postdoctoral programs that I previously mentioned, which did not offer me any financial remuneration, but enriched my knowledge and skill base to a large extent. In my first year out of school, I also enrolled – as I mentioned before – in several graduate courses, and since sex therapy was one of the areas that I planned to specialize in, I also attended a three-day workshop offered by the legendary Masters and Johnson in New York City. This is a treasured experience to me.

So, about 18 months after I had passed the College of Psychology exams and taken all of those additional courses and workshops, I was not intimidated when one of my community college students approached me, at the end of our course, and insisted on coming to see me for marital therapy. I did not feel ready to start a practice, and tried to refer her to another psychologist, but she insisted. Having studied with me for a whole semester, observing my behavior, and becoming aware of my views, she requested to be seen by me, and while not feeling 'ready' yet, I was aware of all the postgraduate programs and courses that I had enrolled in, and so I agreed. My private practice has been ongoing to this day. In the next section, I will outline some tips, insights, and wisdom that I have been blessed to acquire along my professional career.

PART 2: BEING A PSYCHOLOGIST: HEALING, TEACHING, AND RESEARCHING

In this section, I will present a collection of insights and lessons that I have learned in my 35 years of practice. I will divide it into three subsections: research, teaching, and practicing psychotherapy. One area that I will not focus on, in this book, is assessment. Assessment is becoming more frequently utilized in exploring people's personality, their aptitude, their intellectual abilities, and their ability to adapt to the society and world around them. It deserves a more in-depth coverage that this book can provide

Chapter 9

RESEARCH

You cannot get to the top by sitting on your bottom.

Proverb

RESEARCH IS ALMOST ALWAYS MORE COMPLICATED, UNFORESEEN, AND TAKES LONGER THAN PLANNED

Psychology, being considered a science, is based on research which can demonstrate what works and what does not, which techniques help and whom. Research, as you may know after years of being exposed to it during your academic journey, is complex and needs to be well planned. The background upon which you will rely in developing your research question must be thoroughly examined, and the variables you choose to explore must be carefully selected. This takes a lot of preparatory time spent consulting with colleagues who are familiar with the field you plan to research, with research methods and design, and who are ready to offer a helping hand. Sometimes, you can find co-researchers this way.

For instance, you may initially decide to explore a phenomenon in one direction, and end up going in another. That is normal and happens often, so expect it to occur. When you begin to execute your research plan, you will meet all sorts of minor or major challenges: research assistants may not do what you hired them to do, or may simply abandon ship regardless of what they initially promised you; participants may not cooperate, or may even be difficult to handle; and the data you collected – especially if it was collected via questionnaires – may be incomplete.

Once your data are collected and catalogued, completing analyses and drawing conclusions may be a long, tiresome, and frustrating process. New or different analyses may be required, and the results that you were hoping and were even 'sure' you would get may not materialize. Then comes the writing of the article that you plan to publish, but more on that later.

These are but some of the trials and tribulations of doing research. I mention it since you need to be prepared to handle them, and know that you are not the only one who encounters them. Nevertheless, despite these trials, they cannot diminish the thrill of doing research if it is well planned, executed and analyzed and then written up. If you like some surprises, being unsure of results, and the feeling that, while something is challenging, you can do it, and do it well, then research is for you.

WHAT TO RESEARCH: FINDING AN AREA THAT 'NEEDS' YOUR CONTRIBUTION

I am not sure how other researchers choose 'their' area, but it is my impression – from talking with them or reading personal accounts – that some (often the more 'famous' ones) choose it because it spoke to them; it touched them in some way. Three famous examples come to mind in terms of how topics (and not just research areas) are chosen. Alfred Adler was physically challenged, and his walking difficulty was quite obvious. He had also converted from Judaism to Christianity. These were two major issues, amongst others, that made his need to be accepted and valued and his reliance on social transactions the cornerstone of his personality theory. In his theory, he emphasized man's relation to society and his idea that we compensate for our shortcomings, like he did with his physical challenges.

Albert Ellis was another giant who originated the concept of cognitive behavior therapy. It will not, I presume, be sacrilege to point out that he was not a tall man, was never considered to be good looking, his voice quite squeaky, and his demeanor was less than pleasant. Consequently, as an attempt to overcome deflating thoughts that could have overwhelmed him, he developed Rational Emotive Behavior Therapy, (REBT) which is geared to changing how we think and act in situations that may be unpleasant, frightening, or may challenge the picture that we have of ourselves. To wit, he related two incidents that demonstrated how his theory had helped him in everyday life. One was his shyness and lack of success with women. He decided to confront his shyness by taking a ride in the New York subway and standing up at each station and – to the surprise of his fellow travelers – announce the name of the station. His shyness vanished after a full day of doing so. Ellis decided to confront his difficulty of relating to women romantically, by challenging himself to approach 100 women for a date, regardless of how many of them would agree to date him. Ninety-nine did not cooperate, but regardless, Ellis had no more problems with approaching women.

One last example is Viktor Frankle. He survived the harrowing German concentration camps where prisoners who were not killed by the Germans often still died. After the war, wanting to understand why he and others did not perish, he developed his logotherapy, which addresses the meaning our lives have as our primary driving forces. In other words, as Nietzsche proclaimed, "If there is a *why*, there will be a *how*."

While the above examples relate to whole theories, I believe that chosen areas of research are no different. When I 'got into' loneliness, my colleagues were convinced that I had some unfinished business with loneliness, or simply 'suffered' from it chronically. The truth was different. I was in my 30s then, starting my professional career, and having occasionally experienced my own and witnessed my clients' loneliness, I realized that at that time – 35 years ago – loneliness was a virginal path with not too many travellers on it. I jumped in with both feet and never looked back. If you plan to concentrate only on research or, like me, to conduct research along with teaching and clinical practice, you have got to have your heart in it. Usually, this cannot happen while you are a student, since you will often join your professor's research plan in working on what *they* are interested in, and when you do your own research for a thesis or a dissertation, you may not have total freedom, as your supervisor or committee will look over your shoulder, direct and guide you, criticize your work, and require revisions. But once you are on your own, you can let the breeze of freedom kiss your face and confirm that you can now do research on what *you* want, and in the manner that *you* decide.

PUBLISHING IS NOT FOR THE FAINT OF HEART

Research needs to be disseminated to the professional and academic community, and that is done by writing about it in the APA style and publishing it in a professional peer-reviewed journal. Research is of prime importance in psychology, and as such it has become the yardstick by which instructors are evaluated on their way to academic promotions.

There is no question about it – you will face rejection, and as I did once (thankfully only once), you may also receive a demeaning or even humiliating review by some reviewer who has forgotten, or never acquired, social graces. If you cannot stand the heat, get out of the kitchen, or do not even get in there in the first place. Your task is to minimize the number and frequency of these rejections. So, after I had written a paper, I would spend hours in the library in those pre-internet days, going through countless journals in order to examine their statement of 'purpose', the instructions to authors, and the kinds of articles that they published. I aimed at finding the best fit between my article and the journal. Once I zeroed in on a journal or two, I would check that my article complies with their requirements, and that the articles that they published were on similar topics and of a similar quality to mine. This rigorous work at the front end resulted in fewer rejections, and when revisions were required, they were not overwhelming and did not demand a total rewrite of the paper.

> To be nobody but yourself in a world which is doing its best, night and day, to make you everybody else means to fight the hardest battle which any human being can fight; and never stop fighting.
>
> e. e. cummings

Chapter 10

TEACHING

Success is not the result of spontaneous combustion. You must set yourself on fire.

Reggie Leach

In 35 years of teaching, I have taught graduate-level courses, but mainly undergraduate ones, and so my comments will apply mostly, although not solely, to the teaching that I am most familiar with.

In the beginning, I started my teaching at a community college as I was quite anxious about facing a class and did not want to start to teach at the university level right away. Upon graduation, I decided that I would be involved in all three – offering psychotherapy, teaching, and conducting research – and so teaching was a skill that I wanted to acquire. I started teaching an adult evening class once a week. The course was about psychology, life, love, and loneliness.

About half a decade after having started teaching in that and another community college, and seeing how much fun teaching and learning could be, I realized that I was able to develop a good connection with my students. I was successful at encouraging them to expand their horizons and increase their desire to learn, and after having received very warm and positive feedback, I decided to become a university lecturer.

As I have had to do all along my journey, I knocked on doors, met several psychology department heads, and was invited to teach a course at York University. The first course that I taught there was an Introduction to Psychology course with 300 students attending and a small army of teaching assistants to lend me a helping hand. Standing in front of such a very large class – where I could clearly see only those students who were sitting in the front rows – was quite intimidating. It took me a while to create a good rapport with the students, but once that had been achieved, things progressed smoothly. After several more years of Introduction to Psychology teaching, I 'progressed' and was assigned smaller, more manageable classes in topics such as Personality Theories or Abnormal Psychology, both of which were really fun courses. However, my best and most rewarding teaching experience has been offering a seminar on counseling techniques to 25 fourth-year students. In short, this has been my partial teaching experience, in addition to some graduate courses that I taught on other topics in psychology. Looking back, what did I learn?

1. It was good that I insisted on experiencing teaching in addition to research and psychotherapy, since teaching is personally enriching, rewarding, challenging, and requires creativity and the practicing of theoretical material. Teaching is an art. You may be a very knowledgeable psychologist, and even a good therapist, but a lousy teacher. I learned tremendously while teaching. First, I had to relearn material that I had managed to forget from my own university days. Second, being in weekly contact with youngsters who bring with them youth, a hopeful outlook, some confusion about life and about university, and a keen interest to succeed in university and beyond was an unending source of revelations. The contributions that I was able to make, the knowledge that I shared, and even the quasi-counseling sessions that I offered when students requested to meet with me in my office after class were all deeply gratifying.
2. In some respects, teaching is similar to therapy. As a teacher, I had to find the right language, intonation, timing, and interest level in which to deliver the knowledge that the students were there to receive. When knowledge is delivered in a 'dry', monotone level, students will usually not listen, or even if they do, they will get bored easily. I found that when I applied the material to everyday life and enriched the class presentations that I delivered with humor, films, clinical examples, and (even) poetry, then the students were captivated and interested, and from there, the path to learning the material was smooth.
3. When I delivered presentations, I realized that, just like in therapy, knowledge is one part of the equation, but the ability of

the teacher to connect with the class, create an open and non-intimidating environment, and to be truly interested in them *as people* and not just as learners is essential for transmitting knowledge, leaving an impression, and fostering growth and sometimes even lasting changes.

4. There are various approaches to undergraduate teaching. One is the approach that sees university merely as a continuation of high school, where the teacher is expected to teach the entirety of what he wishes that the students learn in class. So the teacher reads and summarizes all of the 'required' sources and presents in class a summary that the student can then study in preparation for their exams. The second approach, which is almost the opposite of the one mentioned above, suggests that the teacher should not just teach in class what the student can find in textbooks and other assigned sources, but instead focuses on different material and delegates the mastering of textbooks to the students. I hold a different view, which in some ways is a combination of the two approaches presented above. I see my role as someone who is like a host, standing by the door and inviting students to come in and 'taste' the smorgasbord of knowledge that is set up inside. I view my role in these undergraduate classes not as a high school teacher who must ensure that all of the material is covered, but as a *facilitator* who aims to engage, interest, and motivate the students to continue to explore the subject matter and to encourage them to learn more about it. I do so not by seeing each class meeting as a marathon where we are all in a race to cover the material, but rather as a meeting where the students and I – not unlike the famous story about the group of blind people examining different parts of an elephant that they were then asked to describe and, naturally, each described the elephant as the part that they had examined – investigate the various ingredients of the subject matter, highlight their usefulness, connect them to everyday examples in order to liven them up, and find how they relate, depend on, and contribute to the field of psychology. My students' year end written feedback indicates that this approach indeed helps to engage them and motivates them to go and further explore the subject matter on their own.

Appendix A is an expansion of a paper that I previously published presenting my teaching style and how it affects students.

5. Teaching, for me, is a dynamic process, and like therapy, I learn from students and they learn from me, not just from the course material. Once students get to know me and feel comfortable in my presence, they will connect the course material to their lives and discuss it in class. They are assured of confidentiality, as much as it is possible to ensure this, using a 'contract' that we all sign at the beginning of the class in order to keep our discussions (not the course material) confidential. Additionally, students regularly ask to meet during my office hours, and often it is not just the course material that they wish to discuss, but their personal issues, anxieties, and concerns.

Thus, teaching, like therapy, is not a distanced interaction, but an involving, dynamic, and bidirectional one that can foster knowledge, acceptance, and personal growth in both interacting entities.

Chapter 11

Psychotherapy

Life is like a garden. Quite naturally, leaves wither and flowers fade.
Only if we clear the decay of the past, then and there can we really enjoy the beauty of the new leaves and flowers.

Mata Amritandamayi

Psychotherapy has always intrigued me. It involves complex, sophisticated attempts to decipher the human mind and ease its pain. The required intimacy between client and healer, who often shares the client's most inner secrets and wishes, and the knowledge that a troubled past, emotional scars, and various fears do not have to define us, has always made me feel curious and empowered. So, I consider myself very fortunate that, after 45 years in psychology (eight as a student and the rest as a therapist), I still feel so enthused and in awe of what therapy can do – for both the client as well as the therapist.

Why do People Choose Psychotherapy as Their Profession?

Some choose psychology believing that there is a lot of money in it. They will be bitterly disappointed to discover that it is utterly untrue. If they become truly good therapists, they will be able to live well and not be haunted by constant financial troubles; however, you cannot become rich from psychology. Others may believe (mostly unconsciously) that if they could help others resolve their emotional pain and traumas, they will find peace from their own emotional stormy seas. These, too, will be greatly disappointed, and moreover, may actually become bad therapists and, under some circumstances, harmful therapists who end up being motivated, directed, and guided by their own pain and fears. Another group, being influenced by movies, are seeking a profession where you can sit for a whole day, listen half-heartedly to clients, and occasionally say, "Aha, aha," then collect your money. As soon as you become acquainted with psychology in undergraduate school, you will quickly realize how ludicrous this view is.

The ones who are likely to succeed are those who love and deeply care about people. It is the ability to empathize, to truly want to understand another person and the ability to listen, support, and comfort that are required for this profession. You may be lucky and be born with this outlook, but most therapists simply learn and develop these qualities and characteristics along the way. However, someone who feels unmoved by others' pain and who does not want to 'be bothered' with others' concerns should certainly look for another vocation.

Assuming it is doing its job, university gives you the basis, theoretical understanding, and some 'tools' that you will need to acquire in order to be able to graduate and to start navigating the road of helping and healing. I found that only by working, being supervised and learning from my mistakes did I become familiar with doing psychotherapy and accumulate the experience, bits of wisdom, and valuable techniques that enabled and empowered me as a therapist.

APPROACHING PSYCHOTHERAPY

The cornerstone of therapy, as I previously mentioned, is the rapport and therapeutic relations that the therapist is able to create with the client. Without this relationship, the client will not develop trust in the therapist, will not open up and explore issues that need to be looked at, and may not persevere in therapy. For different clients, and for their varying concerns, maladjustments, and traumas, psychologists choose the appropriate therapeutic technique and practice it within a theoretical framework that is best suited to the client and their particular issues. However, regardless of how we 'do' psychotherapy, it must be 'done' within a good, safe, trusting, and accepting therapeutic relationship.

MY MODEL OF PSYCHOTHERAPY

Over the course of my career, I have been influenced by behavioral, psychodynamic, cognitive–behavioral, client-centered, and existential approaches. In my practice, I tailor the therapeutic approach to my client and to their presenting problem. However, having all of these theoretical influences and tools at your disposal does not really suggest *what* not to do with clients, but how to approach and help another human.

Over the years, I have developed a model that has been very useful as a guide in structuring my therapeutic approach. It includes five stages, but before I outline it, I would like us to become familiar with the last stage, the end result: Change. Everyone who seeks therapeutic help wants some change, be it change in bad habits, stopping a destructive behavior, acquiring new behaviors, stopping inner pain, resolving childhood hurt, or stopping that nagging fear of elevators – in short, changing the present situation that one may be steeped in to a better one. If this was easy, straightforward, and logical, most people would enter any bookstore, buy some self-help books, and viola! Problems resolved. Some problems may, indeed, be helped in that way, but most cannot be. More is needed before we embark directly on change. Prior to arriving at the change stage, my therapeutic approach includes the following:

1. *Awareness*: A person must be aware that something is 'not working or is wrong' in order to be motivated to institute change. One who is unaware that something is wrong or that the disturbance he is experiencing is something that causes him suffering or displeasure will, naturally, not have any need to change. Consequently, once a client 'contracts' with me to work, we always start by working on their awareness. If they lacks it, I help them develop it, and if they are vaguely aware that things could be better, we sharpen their perception and awareness of the issue.
2. *Understanding*: This stage addresses the understanding of what the problem is and what are its causes. Imagine going to the dentist and complaining that one of your upper right teeth hurts. Can you imagine a situation where, without further checking, the dentist asks you to open your mouth, injects anesthetics into your lower left jaw, and extracts three of your teeth? Naturally, this would not pass as good or even acceptable dentistry. Similarly, in order to effect change, we must know what the problem is

(addressed in the awareness stage) and *how and why* it developed. In the dentist example, a tiny amount of decay is treated differently from badly inflamed gums. So, once we have identified what the problem is, we must understand why it is there, and why the person developed it.

I believe that *every dysfunction is functional.* Consequently, we do not wake up one morning and, for lack of anything better to do, develop an anxiety disorder or another troubling problem. I repeatedly found that there is a 'worthwhile' reason for developing such personal problems. I once treated an 18-year-old youngster, 'Jerry', who sought my help for 'writer's cramp'. It was discovered that his right hand was neurologically intact and he was able to use it flawlessly unless he attempted writing, at which point his hand trembled violently, making it impossible for him to write. As soon as we met, it was clear to me that there must be an underlying reason for this condition. Indeed, when he revealed his background, we discovered that as an only child and the apple of his parents' eye, his parents were dreaming of him becoming a scientist, for which he would need to attend university. Jerry was an average student in high school, not particularly good looking, and somewhat socially isolated. The result of that situation was a youngster with low self-esteem who was insecure and trying hard to hide what he perceived as his incompetence. So, in the face of his parents' expectations, he could either go to university and comply with their hopes, or tell them that he was unable to, and deeply disappoint them. Jerry's unconscious found a creative way out of this conundrum. It developed, on his behalf, the said writer's cramp and Jerry seemed as good as he always wanted to be . He would not have to attend university (since writing was an impossibility for him) while still being considered by his parents as their 'good boy' who would please them if he could. Now that we understood why he was so afflicted, our therapy focused on working with Jerry on his self-esteem and on helping him to raise it, and also teaching him some assertiveness training techniques that would enable him, should he so choose, to approach his parents and discuss his reluctance to attend university. Now Jerry had a choice to make: attend university, which he was now able to do, since his writer's cramp had vanished, or let his parents know why he would not be attending university. Further therapy resulted in Jerry's decision to apply for undergraduate studies in literature (not what his parents hoped for), and as far as I know, he did well.

3. *Ownership* is the next stage of therapy. I worked in a correctional center in Canada for 28 years, and was attempting to provide therapy to some inmates who clearly would not be able to benefit from it. One of their most problematic issues was their inability to assume responsibility for their behaviors, to own their problems. One of them told me that society is to blame. If he could have had a well-earning job and a little house, he would 'never' have resorted to crime. Another one, a child molester, told me that he was sexually molested by his father and uncle and therefore he molested other kids. One more example was provided by one of my private practice clients who was caught red handed stealing some small-value merchandise, a candy bar, from a store. He was asked to repay it and was not officially charged. He told me that, as a young child, he had always liked the bag of candies that he would see through the storefront glass pane, but could never afford it. Seeing it again as an adult aroused his anger at having been so poor during his years growing up, and he expressed it by 'confiscating it'. These examples are but a fraction of the causes that some people choose to explain and justify their problems. Only until and unless the criminal from our first example would own his problem could he be helped to understand that the problem was *not* with the little house that he did not have or with the well-paying job that he could not secure, but with his inability to accept that it is *him* who has very high demands from life, low motivation to achieve them, and a crooked sense of justice, which can be summarized as 'if I cannot get it I will simply take it'. The child molester, in my second example, must understand that regardless of what was done to him, it is *he* and *his actions* that are directly responsible for the pain and harm that he caused his victims. Finally, the 'candy grabber' from the third example has to own *his* anger and propensity to immediately act on it. In short, we cannot 'fix' something that is not ours. Only what we 'own' do we have the ability and the right to change, hence the importance of owning our good and bad characteristics, our abilities and our disabilities, our wishes and our shortcomings.

4. *Empowerment*: People seek therapy at a vulnerable time in their lives, when they feel weakened, confused, or unable to decide how to proceed. It is our role as therapists to empower them, make them see their path clearly, and believe that they can indeed change if they want to. We must help them realize that life can indeed be better and influenced by what they will decide to do, and by how they do it. A very empowering message that I commonly give to my clients is, "I am with you! Through trials and tribulations and for as long as you let me – I am with you, with you until you heal or no longer need me." Knowing and realizing that he or she is not alone, forgotten, or forlorn is immensely empowering to a client, in addition to realizing – with my help – the virtues, abilities, and influence that they have on their lives.

Once we have gone through the previous four stages, we get to the stage of change, with the client being ready, willing, and, with my assistance, able to introduce the changes they need. Therapy is, naturally, part of that stage, but going through the previous stages increases the likelihood that the process will come to fruition and the client will benefit.

THERAPY = ACQUIRING CHOICE

The most important change that psychotherapy can create is the gift of choice. Bertrand Russell, the British philosopher, maintained that a man is the sum of his choices. When undergoing therapy, we may end up doing exactly what we did prior to engaging in therapy, but this time doing it by choice. An example will illustrate the importance of choice. 'Penny' was a 38-year-old client of mine who was married and had a three-year-old daughter. She very much wanted to upgrade her family's living conditions, but her husband's earnings were not enough. Her desire was to go to work and contribute to her family's income. However, her agoraphobia prevented her from doing so, and she felt guilty and incompetent. Our therapeutic journey enabled us to address her agoraphobia, which, after a lengthy therapeutic course, was held at bay and enabled her to go out and work. However, as our therapy continued, she was helped to examine her role as a wife and mother, her yearning to 'upgrade' her lifestyle, and her wish to contribute in equal measure to the household economy. Therapy afforded her the opportunity to examine her long-held beliefs, her 'need' to equally contribute to the finances of the house, and how she viewed her role as a mother and her daughter's needs. Penny decided that she wanted to be a stay-at-home mother until her daughter started elementary school, and consequently she *chose* not to enroll in work. What she did not do previously out of fear and inability, she now *chose* not to do for the sake of her daughter and her belief that she would contribute more as a loving mother than as a worker. In sum, it is not what we do that therapy aims to change, but it is *our choice*, our wishes, and our picture of the world that is most importantly influenced by therapy and has, in turn, such an effect on our mental well-being and contentment.

A Rule of Thumb

When I teach psychotherapy, one of the issues that students are frequently worried about is how to make clients talk about the issues that bother them. They are forever tense and uptight, believing that it is their responsibility to see to it that clients explore their issues. I see therapy as a process geared to enabling clients to explore their inner world, with the therapist being the process enabler. I found that people – in general, but particularly in therapy – will almost always talk about what is important to them if they are only given a chance to do so. So by being accepting and non-judgmental of the client, wanting to listen and help, I invariably see clients talking and opening up. It may take some time, but when the client is ready, they will open up and discuss what is really important to them: the pain that brought them to my office. This process never fails. People will *always* eventually talk about what is important to them. All we need to do as therapists is to enable them to do so. Enabling is more than just being accepting and empathetic. Some clients are reluctant to open up or, even worse, are resistant to opening up. Again, it is the therapist's job to help the client overcome their resistance and thus allow them to open up. To summarize, people, especially those in the psychologist's office, desire to and do talk about the important issues in their lives. We need to learn to patiently encourage them to do so.

TO BE, OR NOT TO BE SOMEONE'S THERAPIST

It is a given that we cannot help everyone, we cannot help *all* people with various maladjustments and disturbances. Let us take a quick look at those we *cannot* treat:

a. The ethical codes of the APA and your local college of psychologists prohibit psychologists from practising outside their area of competence. So, putting it bluntly, you cannot see/help/treat a specific disorder or condition unless you were trained to treat it. There are no two ways about this. If you are not skilled at treating a specific population, age group, or malady, then refer the client to someone who is.
b. Each of us has some tender spots, be they childhood wounds that did not heal or present issues we are unable to face or deal with. Those will also necessitate a referral. To illustrate, here are some examples of what my students answered when I inquired as to who they think that they could not work with:

    - Sex offenders – said by a young woman who later revealed that she was molested as a child.
    - Violent men – said by a student who grew up in an abusive home where his father regularly beat his mother up.
    - Highly anxious people – said by a student who underwent intensive therapy to help her deal with her high anxiety level and could not face revisiting her inner nemesis.
    - Lastly, a woman who lost her marriage to infidelity revealed that it would be impossible for her to attempt to help an unfaithful partner.

    Prior personal therapy, knowing and addressing our demons, and being at peace with what happened and did not happen to us could be highly valuable in helping us be available, effective, and helpful to a wide range of people who are in pain for various reasons.

c. We cannot treat anyone under legal age, a feeble-minded person, or any person who cannot independently agree to be treated without their legal guardian's consent.
d. This group includes those people that it is possible to treat, but would no doubt be challenging. Here, we group those with intelligence that is appreciably lower than average, and those who are not psychologically sophisticated or are incapable of benefitting from insight. These two groups may indeed be helped with behavior therapy techniques.

Chapter 12

THE PROCESS OF PSYCHOTHERAPY

> The greatest glory in living lies not in never falling, but in rising every time we fall.
>
> Nelson Mandela

INITIATING

It is almost impossible for one to attend the first session of psychotherapy with a stranger to whom one will bear their soul without a measure of anxiety. I completely understand and empathize with this feeling, and commonly start our first session by asking the client how they feel. Most clients, being aware of messages from their soul and their sweat glands, will discuss their feelings, while to those who attempt to answer nonchalantly, "I'm OK," I say that it not uncommon for people who attend therapy to feel the butterflies in their stomachs and maybe pressure in their heads. I then proceed to tell the client that they have already gone through the two most difficult actions:

1. Picking up the phone to speak with me and make an appointment, and
2. Actually attending it. From now on, it will become less intimidating as we proceed.

    a. I acknowledge that since I will soon hear about the client and their life – thereby setting the stage for what is to come – I feel that it is only fair for me to briefly tell the client about myself. I tell them about my origins (coming from Israel), the various universities I attended from my undergraduate studies to my Ph.D., where I completed my postdoctoral training, and about my teaching experience. All of this helps the client to feel more comfortable; it also lowers the possibility of the client feeling the need to guess and wonder as to who their therapist is, this person that they are supposed to trust and open up to.

b. I then explain to the client how we will work together. For instance, I highlight the difference between the medical model (with its inequality between the suffering, often helpless patients who are facing the omnipotent physician with his pills, medications, and extensive medical knowledge) and the way that I will work with the client (not 'patient'). Practicing psychotherapy, I do not have a magic wand and thus no readymade solutions. I will work *with* the client in order to help them. That is to say that we will work in collaboration, and as my partner, the client has to assume responsibility for getting better, as well as for alerting me should things not be going the way they wished for, or if the technique that I have chosen as a means to help the client is causing them too much discomfort. Such an approach has a calming effect for someone who is anxious, unsure of how things are done in the psychologist's office, or unsure of what will be expected of them.

c. Unlike many clinicians, I do not initiate therapy with the common request, "Tell me why you came to see me." This seems to be a physician-minded approach that is removed and distanced. Not only believing, but knowing that people invariably discuss what is dear and most important to them, I begin by asking that the client to simply tell me about themselves. At times, I am asked, "Anything in particular?" and respond, "You decide. I just want to get to know you." The client starts to describe their roots and life experiences and I inquire about points of interest and those factors that may be relevant to the client's emotional difficulties. Invariably, the client discusses what is troubling them and how it affects their everyday life.

We then discuss the therapeutic ground rules that, first and foremost, deal with confidentiality, except where by law it cannot be kept; days and times of meetings; their frequency, duration, and fees; and my undertaking to be with and for the client over the duration of the therapeutic journey until such time that we, *together*, decide to terminate it.

NAVIGATING THROUGH THE CLIENT'S LIFE

In one of his very interesting books, '*The Gift of Therapy*', Irving Yalom (2002) indicated that his rich therapeutic experience suggested that therapeutic sessions need to be conducted as a continuous session, with each session taking off from where the previous session ended. Langs, a writer who has influenced me quite profoundly, suggested that doing so would not be "flowing" with the client, but could actually be disruptive. I agree with Langs that picking up from where the client and I left off in the previous session would possibly be serving my need for order and continuation, but since a week usually passes between sessions, the client would most probably be in a 'different space' now, with different experiences and concerns from those which they had in the previous session.

Therefore, Langs recommended (and I found this very useful) that we start each session *without memory, desire, or understanding.* Langs recommended that it is advisable that the therapist not fully remember (although all the details may be documented in the client's file) what happened in previous sessions. It is best to be attentive and see what the client wishes to discuss at present. The client could, of course, be dealing with the same issues that they previously addressed, but with this being a new week, they may be experiencing different issues, some of which that may have arisen just prior to our meeting. If so, asking the client to disregard what they may be concerned about or even struggling with so that they can address an issue that *I* think we should talk about may not only hamper our progress, but actually indicate to the client that I am more interested in the 'completion' of their story than in finding out what is happening with them in the here and now.

'Without desire' is a directive that many students find difficult to follow. This directive addresses the agenda (i.e., 'desire') that therapists commonly have while helping their clients. An example could be: I must get a full and complete history from the client, discuss how they developed this disturbance, and then take them through the prescribed path to resolution. I prefer to be with and for my client, and although we are in the same boat rowing towards the general direction of the shore, I follow the client's needs. At times, they may wish to row fast and in the straight and shortest line to the shore, while other clients may wish to row, rest, and revisit the fish colony in the middle of the river, or pick up a flower on a tiny island. The important thing is that we are progressing, and doing so in the right direction towards an eventual resolution. Progressing in their own manner, rather than in a structured and rigid way, provides the client with a sense of control, and allows me to learn about the client and find out what and how they do things, as well as their interests, when I am the other rower in the boat.

'Without understanding' is another directive that is commonly contrary to what most training suggests and most therapists espouse. Counseling students are usually advised to understand where the client is 'coming from', what is troubling them, and how we as therapists can help. Instead, as Langs recommended, we can approach each session *as if* we have no or little understanding, and consequently we will listen intently, be with and for the client, and ready to remain at the here and now without any prior understanding clouding our view of them.

OUR VALUES – DO WE IGNORE THEM?

'Mary' and 'Joe' came to consult me about their troubled marriage. As they explained what and how they encountered difficulties in their interactions, Mary told me that what is most troubling to her is that when Joe gets upset at her, he hits her. "Nothing too serious," she said, "and he never breaks any of my bones." It was clear to me that physical abuse may not only be a major contributor to their relational problems, but also that if Mary happened to say anything in our sessions that Joe did not like, then she would feel it, literally, at home. This may then prevent her from being open in subsequent sessions. At the end of our meeting, the couple expressed an interest in continuing to work with me. I said that I would do so willingly provided that physical violence ceased immediately. The couple made an appointment for the following week, but never showed up.

As soon as we start to get acquainted with psychotherapy – usually in graduate school – we are warned about not imposing our values on our clients. Some even suggest what I think is impossible to do: that in therapy, our values should remain outside the door. I agree that my values are *mine*, and that imposing them on the client does not make for good therapy. However, whether we know it or not, we all have some core central values that are not only dear to us, but that profoundly affect our behavior. For me, spousal abuse is a red flag, a disruptive behavior that may prevent me from helping a person unless they ceases to engage in such behavior while participating in therapy (with my hidden agenda being that therapy will prevent this behavior from resurfacing later on). I would never impose my other, less central, values on my clients, although truth be told, I may sometimes gently steer them towards another important value of mine: interpersonal tolerance, which I believe is a value that is not salient in our culture but is one that needs to be taught, encouraged, and instilled in people for the betterment of the world.

THERAPY AS A MICROCOSM OF REALITY

Some therapists and clients alike attempt to don a mask when they enter the therapy room. This façade is particularly evident, in my experience, in couple therapy sessions and in psychotherapy groups, and it is unsuccessful. Not only is it unwise and unhelpful to do so, but it is practically impossible. We are who we are; you cannot easily slide into an act and remain there. I see it occasionally with clients, and I am cognizant of what they are doing. I maximize my attempts to make them feel at ease and safe, so that they have less of a need to pretend or play a role. To my students, I advise that in the therapy room, they can only be who they are, and for those who may be uncomfortable displaying the same person that the world commonly sees, I recommend that they attend psychotherapy so that the parts of themselves that they do not like can be changed. We can display only who we are, and if we are uncomfortable with this, it befits us to change and improve ourselves.

REFRAMING: THE DELICIOUS LITTLE DEVIANCY

'Ron' came into my office looking sad and dejected. In talking about how he felt, it quickly became clear that his emotional response was, in my opinion, expected and while it did not 'feel' good, it may have been a blessing. Ron had been married for 18 years to 'Linda' and they had two teenaged kids. Lately, Ron said, he had started experiencing 'the blues', feeling sad, with low energy and even low sexual desire. In the discussion that followed, Ron described his lackluster, boring, and non-involving marriage. He and Linda had grown apart, but continued to walk the path like two well-trained cows that know where they are supposed to go, but not why. I then said, "I am so glad, Ron, that you have the blues!" and smiled, seeing his astonished look. Ron wanted to know why I had reacted in this way, and I explained, "Look Ron, your brain decided to continue and walk the path despite your unhappiness, being unfulfilled, and your disinterest in your partner. But your soul is alive, is watching over you, and has better reasoning abilities than your brain. Via the sadness it – the healthy part of you – is indicating that you are living in dissonance. On the one hand, you are unhappily married, but then you remain in such an unnatural and unhealthy situation, for whatever reasons. Your soul or core seek consonance, and being unable to find it, it indicates that you are in an unhealthy situation. Do you wish to explore it with me?"

By that I was able to:

1. Normalize Ron's sadness, and help him accept it, rather than being ashamed of it and attempting to ignore it, and
2. Help him see that his sadness is a wakeup call to change his situation and make it better in whatever way suited him.

'Nadya' was a 24-year-old, first-year biology student at a local university who came to see me when she started to experience stomach pains and an urgent need to use the toilet whenever she was in a car. Medical tests and a check-up were unable to find a somatic cause for her complaint. Discussing the situation with Nadya, we discovered that she had lost her license after she was involved in a serious car accident some five years ago. While she escaped unscathed, her mother's car was totally destroyed and Nadya, despite the inconvenience of having no driver's license, did not rush to regain one after the two-year suspension period had ended. Recently, she and her husband had moved to the country, and the need for a driver's license became more acute. Nadya's family pressured her to get one, and this resulted in Nadya's pain that occurred when she was in a car, and served as a reminder that she should get a license *only* when she was ready for it, regardless of her family's pressuring. Therefore, something troublesome that she was experiencing came to be viewed differently, as a reminder that 'every dysfunction is functional', indicating that she was not yet ready to drive. Shortly thereafter and following therapy, Nadya stopped having these troubling stomach pains and started to plan how she would go and get her license back.

Reframing is a well-known and frequently used therapeutic technique. It is based on the assumption that the manner in which we view a situation influences how we think, feel, and behave. Similar to Albert Ellis's formulations, it is suggested that when the frame or way of explaining and understanding a situation is changed, its meaning may be dramatically altered (Watzlawick, 1978). Utilizing reframing easily and spontaneously requires that the therapist's cognitive frame is agile and that their ability to consider alternative explanations to a given situation is something that they can do seamlessly.

I frequently utilize reframing when I offer therapy as well as in my personal life, to great benefit. The benefit is not only cognitive (thinking about the situation differently), but also emotional, in that by viewing and interpreting the situation differently, we feel differently about it, and consequently behave differently based on our reinterpretation of the situation. It is a delicious little 'deviant' trick that may go a long way in helping reorient us!

THE THERAPEUTIC RELATIONSHIP

I once saw a caricature with six telephone stands (reminiscent of the pre-cell phone days). One telephone stand had a cross on it and showed a young, well-dressed man talking on the phone. The second phone stand portrayed a Star of David on it and a woman talking. The third one showed a young child who could reach the phone only with the aid of a stool. Standing by the fourth one, was a half-dressed Indian yogi adorned with some Urdu writing. By the fifth stand was what appeared to be someone dressed in traditional Muslim clothing, while by the last stand, which was adorned with hearts, was a beautiful, sexy woman talking – I leave it to your imagination to decipher what she may have represented. What caught my eye was the line underneath this caricature: 'If you want to call God, it makes no difference which telephone booth you use'. If you change the words 'God' to 'client' and 'telephone booth' to 'theoretical orientation', this indicates what, for me, is the essence of therapy: no matter what your theoretical orientation is, the therapeutic alliance that you establish with the client is the most influential and important ingredient that will make all of the difference.

SOME OBSERVATIONS ON THERAPEUTIC RELATIONS

a. The therapeutic relationship holds both a promise and a threat for the client. On the one hand, they are with a therapist, whom they can count on to help them change, but on the other hand, they will open up and thus expose their weaknesses, conflicts, and fears, and this could be quite intimidating.

b. Both participants – the client and the therapist – are influenced by psychotherapy, and their behavior is determined to a great extent by the other's reactions. Psychotherapy is, by definition, first and foremost geared towards helping the client change, but, as in any intensive human interaction, the therapist is affected by the client, their story, struggles, and eventually triumphs. I can recall numerous examples where I was touched and even changed by my clients and the issues that they were struggling with. I have learned from people's grief and how they eased it, how illnesses can affect life, and how we can live and thrive despite pain and disability. For example, I was astonished to find kindness and deep caring between lovers who had broken their union but remained sensitive and supportive of each other. Most of all, witnessing another person's pain made me greatly appreciative of my own situation, making my life seemed like smooth sailing, comparatively speaking.

c. A good, open, and nourishing therapeutic relationship can be fostered by a deeply caring therapist who can be trusted by the client and who does not dominate the client's life. Rogers, the well-known and regarded theoretician, advances the idea that good therapeutic relationships require the therapist to exhibit three essential characteristics: *unconditional positive regard*, which means the unconditional acceptance of the client as a person, even if the therapist does not condone their behaviors; *genuineness and authenticity*, the second 'ingredient' of good therapy, requires a therapist who is being themselves, and not as one who is in the 'role' of being a therapist, and a therapist who is sincere, real, and congruent with their inner feelings; lastly, the most important therapist's characteristic is *empathy*, meaning that the therapist knows where 'the client is', and lets them know that the therapist is with them, understands where they 'coming from', and can connect with them on an intimate level.

d. The client's relationship with his therapist is so central and important that many theorists see it as the key to any influence that the therapist may have on the client. Social psychology and common sense illustrates that the connection between people determines how and whether they can influence each other. I know that regardless of which theoretical orientation I utilize, influencing the client, which is what therapy is all about, will best be achieved if the client can trust and feel at ease with me, appreciates my opinion, and knows that their well-being is paramount in our interaction.

e. Influencing the client brings me to the power inequality in therapy. My students seem to become queasy when we address this point. They either believe that there is no power imbalance or that the therapist should 'ignore it, so it is not misused'. Therein starts a lengthy discussion where I attempt to show my students that, indeed, there is a power imbalance, and that *ignoring* it may cause its misuse. It is obvious that in a meeting of a troubled, vulnerable person with a knowledgeable professional who is 'hired' to help them, there will be power imbalance. There is nothing wrong with this state of affairs. However, what is indeed important is that this imbalance of power must not cause the therapist to manipulate, impose, or coerce the client. The power of imbalance is an integral part of therapy, and if used sensitively, gently, and benevolently, it can be highly effective in helping the client.

f. The therapeutic relationship is both more and less than a social relationship. It is *more*, in that it exists for the client and focuses primarily on their needs, meaning that it is *not* a reciprocal interchange, while social interaction usually is. However, it is also *less* than a social interaction, since many of the client's needs are not satisfied due to the clearly defined limits and boundaries that are part of psychotherapy. The therapeutic relationship is established in order to explore the client's needs, increase their understanding of themselves, and help them alleviate their problems. In doing so, the therapist does not get their needs met (aside from their need to capitalize on a natural talent, be of help, learn about human behavior, and earn a living), must tolerate the frustration and loneliness of this one-way relationship, and be able to control their own conflicts so that they do not interfere with therapy. Another major difference between therapy and social interactions is that, in therapy, two humans who interact do so with the express goal of helping only one of them (the client), after which time the interaction will be terminated. Thus, the psychotherapeutic relationship is *not* a mutual relationship, in that the needs, interests, and welfare of the client are the focal point and always come first. In contrast to a friend or an acquaintance, the therapist does not inject their own problems and concerns into the relationship, and does not allow their feelings, interests, or needs to determine the course of treatment. This is easier said than done for most people, but as you go through graduate school and experience offering psychotherapy, you will learn how to carry this out. This goes back to Rogers' assertion of 'being with and for' the client.

g. Being a sole practitioner and spending all of your professional time offering psychotherapy can be lonely. This is why I always ensured that, in addition to private practice, I worked in an organization surrounded by other mental health professionals and also taught in university.

Think about it: the goal of psychotherapy is to help the client so that they can stop attending as soon as it is psychologically feasible. However, being exposed to an array of humans who seek your help, you will meet people who are bright, witty, interesting, sexually attractive, and those that you may feel a special affinity towards. In everyday social encounters, when you meet such people that you can connect with, you would like to 'keep them' and be in contact with them for a long time. However, being a psychologist, you are required to do what is actually opposed to human nature – bring your clients (including those that you particularly like and connect with) to the point that they do not need to attend therapy with you any longer. Thus, getting to know some wonderful people and not allowing yourself to 'keep them' is a demanding and loneliness-inducing process. It contradicts our basic nature as humans to stay connected to those with whom we resonate, regardless of how close we became during therapy. This leads us into a discussion of therapy as an intimate encounter.

INTIMACY IN THERAPY

On the street, when you ask those who have not experienced psychotherapy about intimacy and therapeutic intervention, you will hear that therapy and intimacy do not go together, especially not if you equate intimacy with sexuality; but a good, thriving psychotherapy invariably creates intimacy.

Cashdan (1973) described the process that is involved in developing intimate relationships in everyday life, and this may help in conceptualizing the evolution of intimacy in psychotherapy. Cashdan maintained that "the growth of a relationship is an intricate but nonetheless a patterned process. Beginning with a series of hesitant, often clumsy forays, it moves with due deliberateness to the point where both participants respond to one another with confidence and trust" (p. 47). Therefore, the initial phase in the development of a lasting relationship involves a series of exploratory maneuvers aimed at gathering information and getting better acquainted with the other person.

The initial phases of the psychotherapeutic process are very similar. The first several sessions are devoted to data gathering by *both* participants. The therapist attempts to get to know the client, their history, modes of interaction, patterns of problem solving, and the emotional pain that motivated the client to seek help. The therapist aims to get a picture as to 'where the client is at', their needs, and what therapeutic approach may be most beneficial in working with them. At the same time, the client is busy with their own attempts to gather information on the therapist. The client pays attention to the office location, the waiting room, and even the office itself. They note and may reach some conclusions about the therapist by the way their office is set up, the manner in which the therapist greets them, and the way in which the therapist is dressed. The client may be taking note of the *kind* of questions that the therapist asks, their non-verbal behavior and the emotional responses the therapist creates in the client. During this initial phase, ground rules are laid and the participants discuss the nature of the therapy, its duration and frequency, and the time and place of their meetings. Fees are agreed upon and their mutual expectations are discussed.

'Risky revealing' is the next phase in developing an intimate relationship. During this phase, the participants (on 'the street' in a regular social exchange) are placed in a highly vulnerable position, entailing a high degree of trust. This trust can only be built if the revealing partner is assured of confidentiality. Similarly, in the therapeutic relationship, the client is expected – with the therapist's encouragement and support, of course – to bare their innermost secrets, to explore their weaknesses and fears, and to allow themselves to become open and vulnerable, while firmly believing that the therapist will understand, nurture, and care about them and their recovery. This very process develops a feeling of closeness to the therapist within the client. The therapist, while not expected to bare their soul, must put aside their own preoccupations, concerns, feelings, and daily worries, and fully attend to the client and empathize with, understand, and accept the client's feelings, thoughts, and experiences. The communication of genuineness in the therapeutic relationship is highly important and directly contributes to the development of intimacy.

The client's self-revelation in therapy cannot continue endlessly, and therefore the participants in any intimate relationship enter what Cashdan referred to as 'strategies', which help them to develop and maintain ongoing relationships. Strategies are different types of behavior patterns, or roles, which the participants engage in during their interactions. For example, some strategies promote dependence in their partners, while others engage in a helper–helped relationship, and still others encourage and contribute to the growth of their partners. In therapy, the therapist takes the responsibility of structuring the relationship in such a way that will help the client deal with their problems and enables the therapeutic relationship to remain open, honest, and intimate. Rarely do two people strain towards each other in such an intense fashion as in psychotherapy. Where else can the client get an uninterrupted hour of time that is devoted to anything they wish to discuss, and is attended to by another person (the therapist) who is very interested in what they have to say and is attentive, caring, and wishes to do whatever they can to help? The therapist never loses his temper, hardly ever seems unreasonable, and is fully accepting and supportive of the client.

Klopfer (1974) observed that there is "small wonder that often times the emotional feelings involved in therapy rise to a crescendo where either or both parties may be frustrated by the fact that the hour has to end and that both parties must go on to their private lives, perhaps not to see each other for another week" (p. 36). Such a setup may foster not only feelings of love, but sexual attraction as well – two of the most 'dangerous' potential occurrences in therapy. While this may be a natural progression of such an intimate relationship (at least on 'the street'), these developments are the antithesis to therapeutic work and cannot coexist within it. Personal psychotherapy and supervision, as previously mentioned, can be particularly helpful in addressing these naturally occurring, but forbidden, wishes. There are ample examples in the professional literature addressing those issues that are beyond the scope of this book. In highlighting this phenomenon, I wanted to alert you, the reader, to another unnatural position into which psychotherapy practitioners are placed. Not only are you, as a therapist, expected to foster closeness and intimacy, which, very uncommonly, is geared towards the goal of the separation of those involved, but this closeness and intimacy, which is so central to psychotherapy, may bring about – in one or both of you – romantic feelings or sexual attraction, which cannot and should not be realized and satisfied. This has happened to more than one of my clients. I was treating a 50-year-old woman who was struggling with anxiety and whose husband, a physician, became aware that she was suddenly very secretive and was hiding a part of her life from him. He observed her hiding in her room for hours, writing and crying. While I was aware that she may have previously developed some romantic feelings towards me, I believed that we had addressed and dealt with them satisfactorily, but this was not the case.

The husband once asked to meet with me and brought his wife along. What he shared with me in that meeting was shocking. Apparently, his wife had fallen in love with me, and he had found letters that she had written to me that she had never shared with me. In these letters, she described sexual escapades between us that had never occurred. It was a very awkward situation where I had to calm the husband and assure him repeatedly that nothing untoward has ever happened between his wife and myself. I also had to ensure that I could help my client deal with her affection for me, which had by now consumed her. A lengthy and quite complex psychotherapy followed, which at times involved the husband as well.

Fellow Travelers

I think that Yalom's (2002) conception of the therapist and client as 'fellow travelers' is accurate and also represents how I view the client and myself: not as 'the afflicted' and 'the healer', but as two people who are equally involved in a journey that is geared towards helping and easing the client's pain and contributing to their growth.

Support and Empower the Client

While they benefit from the therapist's insights and interpretations, clients seem to most value the support and empowerment that the therapist offers them. There may be quite a lot that the therapist can support, encourage, and empower, such as the client's social skills, intellectual prowess, courage to face their inner demons, willingness to self-disclose, ability to delay gratification, commitment to breaking the cycle of drug or alcohol abuse, willingness to invest in improving their troubled marriage, or their ability to gain insight into their situation. One unexpected example of support is what I offered to 'Susan', who came to see me for her recurring nightmares and insomnia. I congratulated her on her creativity – as expressed through her vivid dreams – and I supported her ability to function so well during the day despite such a poor sleep pattern, something that I am quite certain I myself could not do. I then highlighted Susan's propensity for order, her ability not to leave things in an haphazard state, and her strong will and clear mind, and suggested that since her repeated nightmares indicated issues that may be troubling her and that she was indeed able to exert control of her behavior, she should then set aside some time (not during our therapy hour) to concentrate, write about, and reflect on these troubling issues. We would later explore these issues in therapy. This process made it unnecessary for her mind to deal with her issues at night, and she could thus enjoy a good and refreshing night's sleep. Susan was greatly helped by this process.

THERAPY IS NOT JUST FOR THE OFFICE

Admittedly, most therapeutic meetings occur in the therapist's office. However, since the therapist is required to be sensitive to the client's needs and respective of their wishes, flexibility is needed. For instance, I was once seeing a woman in her 30s who asked me to offer her psychotherapy for her phobia of closed spaces. As soon as she entered my office, she complained of feeling suffocated, tense, and ill at ease. Upon her request, we exited the office and conducted our therapy meetings from then on seated on the grass under a tree. It was a novel experience for me, and left quite an impression on 'Nelly', who not only felt much better outdoors, but also understood that her needs and preferences were important and being attended to.

'Monica' was seen by me for a variety of issues, amongst them existential anxiety, marital difficulties, and serious questions about her ability to be a proper mother to her two teenage children. We met regularly in my office, but once, after about two years of therapy, she entered the office quite distressed and unable to sit down. I suggested that since she was so highly tense to the point that she found it difficult to sit down, we should take a stroll on the side streets near the office, and conduct our session that way. After getting over the surprise at my suggestion, she agreed, and so we walked around the neighborhood, attending to her pressing issues and, on the way, noticing the fresh air, growing flowers, and even greeted some of the neighbors. This was so enjoyable that it was some time before Monica agreed for us to conduct our sessions back in the office.

Naturally, these examples are in addition to outdoor *in vivo* exercises that take place as part of behavior therapy. As such, I once went with an anxious client of mine to a mall that was situated close to my office in order to practice her being out socially. With an agoraphobic client, I conducted a whole session in a car while my client drove. While therapy can take place in a variety of settings, it needs to be done in a manner that attends to and respects the client's wishes and needs and is comfortable and safe for both participants.

CHECKING THE CLIENT'S EXPERIENCE IN THERAPY

'Tom' attended psychotherapy with me for several months in order to deal with his low self-esteem, anxiety, and difficulty in deciding how to proceed in life. Our therapy seemed to me to be somewhat uneventful, and I was concerned that Tom was not getting his 'money's worth'. I was glad when Tom indicated that, within a short time, he would like us to terminate therapy. As I always do, I devoted my last meeting with Tom to reviewing his experience in therapy, asking for feedback from which I could learn and improve. I was taken aback to hear the accolades that Tom heaped on me, and how much our therapy had seemed helpful to him.

Another example revolves around 'Judy', who saw me only once and then, despite making another appointment, called later to cancel our therapy meetings. I was very surprised and asked her to meet with me once more if she wanted, free of charge, so she could explain to me the reason for her opting out of therapy so prematurely. Judy was quite uncomfortable when we met, and when I inquired as to what may have happened to cause her to opt out after a single session, she replied that she would find it easier to continue "if you covered your head with a brown bag." I have never considered myself attractive, but neither did I think that I was repulsively ugly. Apparently, Judy did not think so either. In fact, she had wanted to terminate her therapy because she was beginning to feel attracted to me, which frightened her. Despite my request that we continue and deal with how she was feeling, her therapy was terminated.

These are but two examples that highlight the real need not only to be attentive to the client, but also to periodically and *directly* check the client's experience in therapy. Relationships are complex, and as trained as therapists may be in the nuances of interpersonal interaction, they may miss important information that only a direct inquiry of the client's experience can reveal.

"Do You Ever Think of Me Between Sessions?"

A question that clients sometimes ask, and many times wonder about (as the therapist has many clients while clients only have but one therapist) is whether the therapist ever thinks of the client between sessions. The therapist does not need to wait for that question to be asked, or even pondered about. I, for example, ask clients who have shared with me their anxiety about an upcoming dental extraction to call and let me know how their experience was. Others I ask to let me know how they felt after their daughter left to attend university out of town, or I follow up with those who have shared with me their excitement about an upcoming job interview. I may also periodically say to a client, "As I attended teacher–parent day in my son's school this past week, I remembered how proud you were telling me of all the accolades that you heard from your daughter's teacher when you attended the meet-the-teacher day last month." I also, though infrequently, call clients, particularly if they are struggling with a crisis, are grieved by the death of a loved one, or are about to accompany their child down the aisle.

To Admit or Not to Admit to Your Mistakes

Therapists are fallible humans who, despite their rigorous training, make mistakes. To paraphrase Albert Ellis, the goal should not be to refrain from making mistakes all together, but rather to minimize their frequency and severity. You may make a mistake as a therapist, such as missing an important clue, saying something that was better left unsaid, or initiating a therapeutic technique that does not bear the fruits of success. If the client confronts you, do not deny or cover up your mistake, as this could seriously damage your therapeutic relationship. I would suggest 'fessing up', even before the client approaches you. The chances are that your mistake was noticed by a client who is intensely tuned into your behavior and speech, and your outright admission of a mistake and offering a way of correcting it could not only heighten their respect for you, but also serve as a model of appropriate behavior for them.

THE UNIQUENESS OF EACH CLIENT

While there are a variety of therapeutic approaches, techniques, and clinical skills that can be utilized in attempting to help those who are seeking our assistance, it must be emphasized that standardized approaches cannot and should not be applied, since each person and situation are unique and require an approach that is tailored to their specific circumstances. For example, the field of sex therapy, which I practice, reminds us of the necessity of tailoring our approach to our clients. While there are several tried and tested approaches to addressing males' erectile dysfunction, each case is unique. Erectile dysfunction, or a male's difficulty in getting or maintaining an erection, may have a variety of causes that require different approaches. Among its causes are various illnesses, the side-effects of medications, aging and a lowered testosterone level, a couple's marital woes, low self-confidence and 'spectatoring' (i.e., the man's self-monitoring of his performance, which may bring about sexual dysfunction), fear of impregnating the woman, fear of commitment, or lack of sexual desire. Those are but *some* of the potential causes of erectile dysfunction and, naturally, the therapeutic approach will differ in addressing each of them.

'Rose' sought my help with a persistent problem of lack of sexual desire, which was quite alarming for a 25-year-old woman at the prime of her life, personally and professionally. Rose had been with several boyfriends, but remained single, sad, and doubting her capability to find a mate. Pressure and expectation from her immediate and extended family made her situation even worse. Our therapy started with referrals to her physician in order to rule out medical causes for her problem. The results had come out negative – she was perfectly healthy physically. We then started to explore the history of the events that she had experienced in relation to her sexual functioning. While there could be a variety of reasons that may have caused her condition, in Rose's case, it was her parents' tumultuous marriage that had made her highly concerned that her relationships and sexual encounters would result in as much pain and heartache as her parents had experienced. Her unconscious way to prevent such suffering was to extinguish any sexual 'fire' that may be burning in a woman of her age, and thus 'ensure' that no long-term relationship, and consequent marriage, could be possible. Obviously, the chosen treatment approach in this case would be very different if, for instance, Rose was in a long-term relationship that included sexual activity that was painful for her (and thus her lack of sexual desire protected her from further physical discomfort), or if Rose was not able to reach orgasm without some sadomasochistic activities that she was reluctant to disclose to her sexual partner and thus, rather than engage in sex and so remain 'high and dry', chose – most probably unconsciously – to have no sexual involvement at all.

The Client, Here and Now

The client, as well as the therapist for that matter, is the same person with the same behavior and shortcomings in therapy as in the world. A client who avoids closeness in therapy most probably does so in real life as well. When a client is suspicious, doubtful, or mistrusting in therapy, you will certainly find that they are also like this in general life. A client who repeatedly asks what you mean and how he should do things is certainly unsure of themselves in life as well. We are the same across many situations, react similarly, and act in accordance with our fears, preferences, and tendencies. Consequently, what occurs in therapy is of the utmost importance in reflecting who the client is and what their issues are that they may be struggling with. Therefore, it is so important that the therapist observes and follows the client's verbal and non-verbal behavior during the therapeutic hour in order to gain an understanding of the client as a functioning person, much more than merely collecting historical data.

Self-Reflection

We therapists know or ought to know ourselves, and so we are aware of our reactions to clients and to their behaviors. Those reactions that we have are invaluable sources of information and insight into the client's feelings and internal world. If you, as a therapist, feel bored or excited, confused, or irritated by the client, this may indicate that the client's interactions, verbal messages, or inner world need examining, as they possibly arouse similar reactions in others who interact with them as well.

Self-reflection and knowledge are naturally related to individual therapy. I understand that a growing number of graduate programs require their students to attend personal therapy. While I highly recommend that therapists and therapists-to-be enroll in therapy themselves, I struggle with the notion that therapy should be a *requirement* of these programs. In general, I am reluctant to use coercion in any context, and I believe that attaching a degree to the completion of specific number of required hours of personal therapy is neither wise nor does it guarantee any appreciable benefit when it is done under the pressure of the graduate program, rather than out of free choice. That being said, I still believe that self-knowledge will greatly contribute to yourself personally, professionally, and socially, and as a recipient of so many benefits, you will no doubt become a better and more effective therapist.

THE PROMISE AND PROBLEMS OF TRANSFERENCE

Transference, which Sigmund Freud and, later, his daughter Anna wrote about, is an ingenious tool that can be used to examine the client's inner world and utilize the therapeutic exchange in order to assess the client's painful, traumatic, or alternatively positive past experiences that may be evoked and expressed during the therapy hour.

Therapy, as offered by Freud, had a minimal level of active interaction between the two participants and it was thus assumed and accepted that transference was indicative of past experiences that the client had undergone and needed to be explored in therapy. In this day and age, even Freudian or dynamically oriented therapies rely – to various degrees – on the therapeutic alliance and interaction. As such, it behooves the therapist to reflect on their sessions and check whether there is any possibility that the client's reactions could have been precipitated by what the therapist did or did not do. It would be clinical laziness, in my opinion, to attach all such client behaviors to transference. Without intending to or being aware of it, the therapist may have evoked the client's reactions and, consequently, he must ameliorate the therapeutic interchange in order to bring about changes in the client.

THERAPIST'S SELF-DISCLOSURE

As I went through undergraduate and graduate training in the 1970s, the emphasis was on deflecting any queries the client may have had about ourselves, and answer with a simple question of, "Have you ever experienced that?" with "What do you mean?" or "Why do you need to ask that?" Yalom (2002) mentions the triumvirate of magic, mystery, and authority that healers have maintained throughout history, allowing their patients to drift through the fog that serves to hide the therapist's humanness, creating an aura around them. In his distanced approach from his patients, Freud may have also hoped to create this aura. The 21st century is the age of information. My clients and my students know much about me through the loyal service of the biggest demystifier in human history: Google. So, attempts to hide behind your credentials are fruitless and non-beneficial to the therapeutic process.

Thus, when 'Denise' was highly anxious facing abdominal surgery, our sessions naturally revolved around that big event. She found it very helpful, she later told me, when I said to her, "Denise, I have never experienced general anesthesia and such extensive surgery as you must undergo, but drawing on my experiences of dental and gum surgeries that I have had, I am certain that I would be as anxious as you are now, or even more." This seemingly simple revelation about myself made Denise feel how much I cared for her, and how human and normal her responses were. She opened up, discussing with me the reasons that she was so highly anxious, and went for surgery some weeks later feeling much more relaxed and ready to encounter whatever awaited her.

'Milan' and 'Katerina' were relatively new immigrants from Eastern Europe who consulted me in seeking help for the difficulties in their marriage. Our exploration of their situation revealed that a major part of their stress, which contributed to their marital woes, was related to their troubled acculturation. They arrived in Canada five years earlier with 'Mishka', their six-year-old daughter, who did not want to come to Canada, and missed her friends and mostly her beloved grandparents. They found it difficult to secure permanent positions in their respective fields, and one year into their stay in Canada, they felt obliged to send their daughter back to their country of origin to live with her grandparents. While I could not inherently change their situation, I related to them some of my own experiences as a newcomer to Canada some 15 years earlier. Hearing that I was human, fallible, and vulnerable like them contributed immensely to strengthening our therapeutic alliance and encouraged them to be open, increasing their motivation to address the issues that they needed to work on.

WHAT AND WHEN TO SELF-DISCLOSE?

As I have suggested, and based on my experiences with clients, therapist's self-disclosure can be beneficial. However, this must be done at the appropriate time, and to a degree that will serve its purpose but not leave the therapist's life as an 'open book'. A question that could be helpful when deciding whether to self-disclose is: will this be beneficial to the client? The client is seeking our assistance in improving their feelings and/or relationships, and the therapist's self-disclosure needs to be carried out as an aid to that goal. In general, talking about our own life and experiences is unhelpful in that it takes away precious time from the session. Self-disclosure of experiences and details that are not too intimate and could help the client anchor their experiences and reactions is good and helpful. Usually, experience and supervision are the best tools for learning when and how to properly self-disclose. Since confidentiality in therapy applies to the material revealed by the client and not that which is disclosed by the therapist, it is advised that you do not disclose anything that you do not want to become public knowledge.

FREEDOM: A DUTY AND A GOAL

The existential approach to therapy looks our existence squarely in the eye, and leaves no other conclusion: we are the ones who are responsible for ourselves. We are the authors of our fate and the creators of the narrative that is called 'our life'. This freedom that we have as humans is our duty. We cannot avoid it, and as Sartre put it, "we are condemned" to it. It would indeed be a duty, at least for some people, if we could conclude that we have no free choice, and must allow the sea of life to take us with its waves to wherever it chooses. We could then maybe feel similar to those with an external locus of control – I can be and do as I please because it has no effect on my life. Instead, we play the central role in creating our world. Paraphrasing what Epictetus said more than two millennia ago, and upon whose ideas Albert Ellis based his cognitive–behavioral approach, the world is not what it is, but what we make of it. Every thought, feeling, or action is generated by us. That is an encouraging message – if I do not like my thoughts, my actions, my feelings, or my life, then I can change them. I have the responsibility to ensure that my life goes in whatever direction that I desire, and I may have or need to acquire the means of doing so. Emphasizing this freedom in therapy – with the responsibility it puts on us on the one hand, but also with its almost limitless potential on the other hand – could be very encouraging, enticing, and empowering for us as therapists and for our clients.

Assuming Responsibility

'Derek', a 42-year-old lawyer, came to my office looking dejected, depressed, and hopeless. When I inquired about his condition, he related to me that he had 'severe' marital problems. He could not 'stand' his wife. She felt similarly towards him, and thus, they had not had sex for months. He suspected that she may be falling in love with a man with whom she worked, and he himself was considering a similar 'arrangement'. When I inquired as to why he was still in his marriage, which he described as hopeless, he sadly remarked that his wife had supported him through school, and he felt indebted to her, and thus had to go along with whatever happened, feeling unable to change the situation.

Our therapeutic work focused on encouraging him to take responsibility for his life, empowering him so that he understood that he could introduce the changes in his life that he may have required, he could indeed influence and improve his life, and that each of us, as Kipling wrote, is the captain of their own soul and – I would add – the driver of their life's bus. Several months later, Derek decided to approach his wife and suggest that she could join us in therapy. To his surprise, she readily agreed. Interestingly, her major complaint about Derek was related to his passive approach to life and his not assuming responsibility for its course. Two years of marital and individual therapy followed, at the end of which the two were working together on healing their relationship and improving their marriage.

Assuming responsibility for our lives, hardships, relationships, and lot in life is the most basic requirement we face, whether we are therapists or clients. As Nietzsche wrote, when there is the why, we will find the how.

A Silenced Client

Talk therapy, as psychotherapy is often referred to, arouses an expectation in us that clients will talk, open up, share, disclose, and verbally reveal. Consequently, many are not prepared to deal with a client who does not 'talk'. It is important to note that clients may be silent for a variety of reasons, a partial list of which may include resistance to entering therapy, the fear that people may feel when they are about to explore a particularly painful issue, or it may be the fault of the therapist who, by their behavior, may cause the silence. Each example would require a different approach and I therefore do not like 'patterned approaches' to silent clients.

The following example, which occurred during the first year of my practice as a psychologist in the correctional center, illustrates that silence may have a completely different cause from what we may suspect, and may fulfill a valuable need for the client. A resident, as the incarcerated were called, asked to see me for therapy. Upon starting to meet with him, I went through presenting myself and then invited him to speak. He began by relating how sad and angry he felt, and how much he missed his three siblings, who he was unable to see during his incarceration period. As he was speaking and staring at a faraway dot on the wall (or so it seemed), he became silent and continued to stare for the remainder of the session. The second session was quite similar, with him being mostly silent and me feeling increasingly ill at ease with his silence. Influenced by what I was taught and the psychology books that I had read, I interpreted his silence as resistance, and so in my following supervision session, I consulted with Reg, my mentor and supervisor, and questioned the value of continued therapy with such a 'resistant guy' who would not talk. Reg brought Robert Langs' works into our session, and the 'three' of us agreed that if the client comes to therapy out of their own volition, and *continues to attend*, they must be getting some benefit out of it. The suggestion was to engage the client and guide him into reflecting aloud on his silence.

Upon my initiating such a reflection during the following therapy session, the client expressed his profound appreciation for me 'staying' with him and accommodating his need for a quiet corner. He related to me that, living on a correctional unit with 47 other residents, he was surrounded by noise, constant activity, a blaring radio, and correctional officers shouting their orders. He saw my office as a refuge from all that, a place where he could come, indulge in his private thoughts, and his need to be silent and respected. Needless to say, I was taken aback in recognizing the truth of what he said, and was thankful that I had not ended his therapy. Two sessions later, he came in and, knowing that I cared enough to let him be quiet, he started talking about the issues that he was struggling with, and kept on talking for many sessions to come. Once more, silence may mean many things, but before you react, find out what the silence is about.

It is Easy to 'Destroy' a Client

'Cheryl', a previous student of mine in an evening adult class, called after the course ended to ask for therapy with me, saying, "I got to know you in class, and I feel comfortable speaking with you."

Cheryl was a 50-year-old divorced woman with two teenaged daughters who was struggling financially, socially, and romantically. She had no partner at the time. She seemed so helpless and hopeless, and she related to me that her deep sadness had also been related to something that had happened ten or eleven years earlier. Cheryl had two young children, both two years old at the time, and she was freshly separated from her verbally abusive husband, and was feeling quite desperate. She sought psychiatric help after an incident in which she was driving in a mountainous region with her two noisy young kids, and out of desperation had an urge to cause the car to roll over and kill all three of them. The psychiatrist whom she consulted sat behind a "huge desk and I was seated on a low chair," which immediately felt intimidating to her. Upon hearing of her thoughts during that trip, her psychiatrist proceeded to "shred me to pieces," indicating that she was insane, and that had she come to him right after the event, he would have hospitalized her. Cheryl left his office sobbing, desolate, and humiliated. She never again wanted to see a mental health professional. Cheryl became anxious as she discussed this event with me, even a decade after the unfortunate occurrence, looking intently at me for any signs of anger or disapproval.

I was indeed angry, but not at Cheryl. I was angry at the careless and insensitive psychiatrist, and shared with Cheryl my feelings while seeking to assuage her pain by normalizing her feelings (although not her wish to kill herself and her children). "You know, Cheryl," I said, "each of us has a breaking point, and it seems that your loneliness, fear, financial concerns, and very demanding young children brought you to yours. It would, of course, have been a tragedy had you acted on your impulse, but I can fully understand what caused it as we all have sometimes desperate thoughts when we feel frightened or 'caged'." My reaction, which normalized Cheryl's desperation, did wonders for her. It was as if a heavy burden that she had carried on her shoulders was lifted at once. She was clearly relieved.

Please beware of how you react to what clients tell you. They trust and confide in you, and give you tremendous power to affect their lives. Build, do not destroy; empower, do not humiliate.

DREAMS

Freud made us aware of the importance of dreams as the "royal road to the unconscious." Dreams are seldom ways to decipher what may be bothering us, and as Yalom (2002) indicated, they are "cryptic, extravagant and heavily disguised" (p. 225). Like many others, I have made the acquaintance of the myriad of popular books that attempt to simplify dreams and give the various themes a unified description, such as 'fish means a lot of money', and other such silly blanket statements. Dream analysis is a complex endeavor that needs to be mastered before it is offered to clients. While Freud naturally analyzed dreams relying on a psychodynamic principle, it is obviously not the only way to conduct dream analysis.

Let me illustrate how dreams could contribute to therapeutic work in addition to providing the client with the message that the therapist understands him. 'Peter', a 28-year-old computer analyst, came to see me for a general feeling of malaise. Peter was not very descriptive of his situation, perhaps because he worked in solitary conditions on 'building' computer programs, and so did not need to use his verbal skills very often. Our initial session was guided by some questions that I asked him in order to learn a bit about 'Peter the person'. At the end of that meeting, I suggested that, starting with our next session, I would do more listening, giving Peter center stage. Peter arrived 10 minutes late to our next session the following week and was visibly feeling 'down'. When we started the session, he mentioned that he had been having a troublesome dream that I encouraged him to share. In his dream, he was walking across a large piece of land when suddenly he almost tripped into a hole out of which crabs, snakes, and cockroaches were emerging. When we closely examined the dream, Peter realized that it signified his great concern about all his weaknesses, dark secrets, and flaws that therapy may unearth.

Sharing this dream with me, especially when he was not otherwise verbally articulate, allowed me to help Peter understand that I would be *with him and for him* throughout the process, that he would have control over what issues to bring up, and that this would help him deal with anything that caused him discomfort. It was immensely helpful for our therapeutic work, and strengthened our therapeutic alliance and his trust in me.

Occupational Hazards

When the public envisions a psychotherapist's office, they commonly imagine an air-conditioned, cozy place, with nice furniture in a professional office building with the therapist seated comfortably and listening attentively to their client. What often goes unnoticed are the so-called 'occupational hazards', amongst which are:

a. *The loneliness and isolation* that may be experienced, especially by those who practice solely as independent practitioners.
b. *The intimacy dance.* In their professional life, the therapist engages in intimate interactions with clients, which end at the termination of the therapeutic hour, only to restart with the next client several minutes later, and with the same client again the following week. This on-and-off 'intimacy dance' is demanding, requires much self-control, demands intimacy without getting sucked into the client's life and worries, and is – naturally – insufficient to support the therapist's emotional life.
c. Being surrounded by *clients who may appreciate, adore, or even idealize* him, the therapist may forget or become less appreciative of their own family members and friends, who may become less enamored with us and more aware of our human failings.
d. *The stress of unending therapy.* Clients come and go, but the sole practitioner is basically on a merry-go-round of seeing needy, defeated, desperate, confused, or 'lost' people who need the therapist to be strong, focused, creative, and able to help them. While gratifying and enriching, this can also be quite grueling, demanding, and exhausting.
e. *Client's behavior*, especially that of those who are in danger of attempting suicide, displaying aggressive or threatening behavior toward the therapist, those with little motivation to change, and the ones who terminate therapy prematurely, adds to the therapist's stress, and so we need to constantly observe, monitor, and predict potential problems and prevent them.

f. *The therapist's personal attributes.* The very traits that are required to do the work of a therapist are the same ones that may create high levels of stress in therapists: high idealism, empathy, independence, a need to nurture and help, and also a need to be needed. Consequently, when a therapist faces any of the following situations, it may have more of an impact on them than if they did not possess those attributes: seeing clients that the therapist does not like; treating too many clients; being unable to ease a client's pain; self-doubts about the therapist's ability to help; conflicts with colleagues; over-identification with clients' concerns at work; and sexual attraction from/towards a client.

These occupational hazards, which are not uncommon in therapists' experience, should not deter us from caring, empathizing, or conducting therapy. Every profession has its own set of occupational risks, and as such, there are a variety of ways of dealing with them, which this book will not address. However, being cognizant of them and of their effects on us may help us to prepare for and prevent them. As a therapist, I suggest that you prepare, be vigilant and do not neglect yourself, such that you can avoid the depression, recurrent physical illness, loneliness, alcohol and drug abuse, or hostility towards clients and/or colleagues that are signs indicating that you did not do a good job in preparing and attending to your own needs. This is referred to as 'burnout'.

Epilogue

PERSONAL GROWTH AND RICHNESS OF EXPERIENCE

In this book, I have briefly outlined what it takes to go from high school to graduate school, and some points of reference regarding therapy. I strongly believe that if there is a *why*, we will find the *how*, and if there is a will, there will be a way. It is our responsibility as humans to chart the course of our lives and to go down the path that will lead us to the goal we envision for ourselves. University is not an easy experience and, to be honest, I eagerly waited for it to conclude so that I could do what I really desired – be a clinical psychologist. Being focused, determined, and committed is the guiding principle in my life. That is how I completed my studies and developed a thriving private practice in addition to a full time job in a jail, while also teaching in university and conducting research. I do not only believe, but I *know* that we are the authors of our life's story, the masters of our fate. I previously mentioned the stress and occupational hazards that we may encounter while being psychotherapists. In closing, I would like to briefly discuss the richness of that experience and the consequent personal growth that I have enjoyed.

    a. *Psychology as a calling*. For me, this is what 'doing' psychology has always been. You cannot get rich from helping others, nor do I believe that it is morally right to acquire wealth due to others' misfortune. If caring, empathy, and a sincere wish to help others do not burn within you, then maybe this profession is not meant for you. I chose this profession and scaled many walls because it seemed that I was meant to do it, always wanted to do it, and 35 years after graduating with a Ph.D. in psychology, I am still very excited about the field and it's potential.

b. *I have met some wonderful people.* It is a question that I get asked occasionally: "Do you like all of your clients?" The answer is, "Not necessarily." Some clients I am neutral to, some I like, and some I like a lot. My years of practicing as a clinical psychologist have offered me the opportunity of meeting some truly wonderful people, many that I learned a lot from and was inspired by. It saddened me that I could not ethically befriend them, but I was immensely grateful that they happened to walk down the same path with me, at least for a while.

c. *I shared the world of many.* Being a psychotherapist is magical. It allows you to be invited into another's world, their life stories, and their accumulated wisdom. I learned about struggles that people endured through no fault of their own; of the incredible effects that parenting has on us, of people's ways of running away from responsibility, of the resiliency of the human spirit, and of triumphs that made my heart sing. I heard uplifting stories, saw unshakable faith, and picked up some good jokes to boot!

d. *I learned and grew.* It is impossible to be so intimately connected to clients, enter their world, listen to them, and navigate stormy seas with them and not feel enriched, get new ideas to make one's personal life better, or gain appreciation of one's good fortune at not facing larger and more daunting obstacles. While doing therapy, I learned quite a lot from those courageous souls whose personal space I shared for a while.

e. *I not only believe, but I know, that I am better for it.* I know who and what I was prior to spending more than three decades with my clients, and when I look at myself today, never for a minute do I intend to suggest that there is no more work that I need to do on myself, but my task would be so much more daunting had I not had my clients to grow with. I met amazing people, including clients, other psychologists, and students. I am certain that they have also benefitted from our interactions, but I am wholeheartedly thankful for what I got out of them – a richer, more invigorating, and more mindful existence.

A musician must make music, an artist must paint, a poet must write, if he is to be ultimately at peace with himself. What a man can be, he must be.

Abraham Maslow

Appendix A

COUNSELING PSYCHOLOGY: TEACHING THE THEORIES EXPERIENTIALLY[*]

> When you were born, you cried and the world rejoiced; Live your life in such a manner that when you die the world cries and you rejoice.
>
> Siegel, 1991; p. 224

INTRODUCTION

It has been ten years since I started teaching this fourth-year undergraduate course in psychology. Students' feedback indicated that they found the course unique and very engaging, differently structured from the other courses in which they enrolled, and experientially delivered. The amount of endorphins that I secrete after every class meeting, the almost perfect student attendance throughout the school year, and the kind and encouraging feedback from students at year's end all motivated me to put on paper what takes place in the class. Since paper is a flat medium and limited in size, this description can, at best, only be a unidimensional reflection of the rich, enticing, and engaging class meetings that my students and I have repeatedly created. I was fortunate to have previous students in this course contribute their impressions of and experiences in this class.

---

[*] Parts of this appendix were previously published in the *Psychology and Education Journal*. Reproduced with permission.

Mary

Several months have passed since I finished Ami's course, but its impact on my life has grown since I walked out of our classroom for the last time. I look on this class with a degree of fondness I never quite developed for any of my other university courses. What always surprised me upon completion of my other classes was how quickly I forgot what I had been taught. Sitting in large lecture halls, furiously taking notes, my presence unnoticed by students and professors, made most of my courses far from impactful. It is with hesitation that I admit that my university career was riddled with an excess of hours that were spent in classrooms that had very little consequence on the person I am. But Ami's class was different. Though it was rich in detail and theory as my other courses were, I can vividly recall so many of our classes together. I remember them because I experienced them.

Thinking back on this class, my mind is flooded with memories of guest-speakers, intimate disclosures by many of my peers, and moments in which I was enthralled with the depth of what I was learning. Ami's class was one I looked forward to, though it fell at the end of one of my most tiring days each week. I didn't just attend this class, I escaped to it. Here was a room full of strangers who quickly became friends, and a professor who transformed into a mentor. Here was a class in which I did not have to struggle to retain the information, for I was learning life lessons. Here was a place I could learn with my hands and my voice and my heart, as well as my mind. Here was a course that truly changed my being and my world.

The class is composed of up to 30 fourth-year undergraduate students who are mostly quite knowledgeable about psychological theories and are highly motivated to have some 'hands-on' experiences. Such a small class is necessary to foster the cohesion, safety, and sense of intimacy that are commonly shared in the class.

Sally

Intimacy: a word I never associated with any aspect of education within a higher-level institutional setting. A teacher is someone to be listened to and to learn from, not an individual with whom an entire class of students could feel a connection. At least, this was what I believed until I was fortunate enough to end up in the class that this paper describes. With a foundation built upon a small class size, this peer-to-peer and professor-to-student sense of camaraderie and security was strengthened over the academic year, through various means. To name just a few, the professor (who preferred to be called by his first name, Ami) took the time to learn each of our names and encouraged us to introduce ourselves to everyone in the room.

All of the lectures I attended, prior to 4th year, were held in classes with a seating capacity for well over a hundred students, most of which were filled. This arrangement made it virtually impossible for professors to know, and much less to remember each of their students' names; knowing only a handful by name and only because those individuals stood out, in some way, from the remainder of their peers. This was also the case with interactions between students, who recognized only a handful of their peers and were on a first-name basis with even less. Such anonymity promoted feelings of detachment and boredom. In contrast, when you walk into a room where everyone knows and acknowledges your presence, the notion that you are an important member of the class is confirmed and you find yourself looking forward to your weekly meetings there.

In this counseling course, with fewer than thirty students, we were given the opportunity to get to know one another, and eventually there were no strangers. This enabled us to talk about ourselves and listen (giving our full attention) to others in the class.

Research has indicated that integrating course material with personal growth and counselor development results in a clearer understanding of the material, and this is a main component of the psychosocial development of counselors-to-be. Thus, students were afforded the opportunity to both learn psychological concepts and counseling skills, while also applying those concepts to their own experiences and life situations (see Miller, 1997).

Sally

Some learn visually, by reading and observing. Others perform best after auditory stimulation, by listening and participating in discussions. Personally, I have always been one whose memory was best strengthened through emotional involvement. When I can integrate the information to be learned with something that I have personally experienced at some point during the course of my life, not only is my understanding crystallized, but also the material becomes more substantial. A theory is transformed from a trivial list of 'things' that must be memorized, to a concept that has form and depth; something with intrinsic value.

Before this course, university existed for me as little more than a chore, or work if you will. As a result of my years as an undergraduate, I did not feel as though I had grown as a person. I read articles and memorized charts, prepared for tests and expanded my knowledge of matrices and vector calculus; all of which I could have done alone from a textbook. My experience was vapid and tolerated primarily out of necessity for future vocational goals. However, this counseling class was an exception. The teaching in this class was experiential. Psychological concepts were presented and then through various activities we were able to apply the concepts and theories to ourselves (and in 'self' I am referring to the Freudian depiction of 'the center of consciousness'; the sum total of one's thoughts, feelings, and sensory impressions which come about as a result of our life encounters).

This counseling psychology course gave students the opportunity to learn some counseling skills and increase their knowledge of interviewing and listening skills, introspection, insight development, and appropriate self-disclosure. *Appendix B – How to Make the Most of this Class, or ROPES* illustrates some suggestions as to how students can maximize their benefit from attending this course. The students read it, and we then discussed it.

Sally

We, as students, generally understand that it is expected of us to participate during classes. Over the years it becomes almost intuitive knowledge that we must be open to explore and consider new paradigms, treat people with respect, as well as to take responsibility for our behaviors and the course of our learning. Even if by trial and error, most of us come to understand that no one is going to hold our hand through university. All of these points were reiterated to us through the concise acronym 'ROPES': Responsibility, Openness, Participation, and Sensitivity. However, it contained one more point (the 'E'), which many of us often forget in the midst of routines: Experimentation!

When we were looking over this in our first class of the year, I was almost transfixed by the very word. I could not recall the last time I had actually tried to change my behaviors to experiment with ones contradistinctive to the norm. Oh sure, I had thought about altering certain aspects of myself in this regard, but nothing ever materialized from it. Somehow, seeing this acronym on paper in front of me, and discussing it in class served as a sort of mental thrust, perpetuating me into motion. Over the course of the year I succeeded in self-disclosing events of my life that I had never before dreamed of and from this I was able to generalize the behavior outside the classroom and be more open with friends and family.

Mary

ROPES caught my attention immediately. By handing us this sheet of guidelines, Ami had made it clear from the first class, that we were all expected, and encouraged, to become active members of his class.

It was the 'E' that I took the most to heart. It stood for 'experimentation', and encouraged us to try to respond with new behaviors in class. Ordinarily, I enjoy answering questions and being vocally involved in classroom discussions. But this part of ROPES suggested trying to conduct myself differently at times. While I still maintained my usual responsive self much of the time throughout the rest of the year, there were classes in which I experimented. When Ami would ask a question that I knew the answer to, I would sometimes wait and watch and listen. It fascinated me how this small change in my participation gave me such a new perspective. By periodically choosing to be silent, I was able to witness my classmates engaging heavily in the material. I learned new perspectives with which to view a question. I gained an intense respect for many of my peers, when I attempted to be slow to speak, and quick to listen.

This experimentation soon generalized to my interactions outside of our classroom. True to the nature of a counselor-to-be, I began to try to listen more to the people who shared my world. Much to my delight, learning to experiment with my behaviors has helped to change the way I approach my relationships. Ami told us several times throughout the duration of the course that people will always, eventually, talk about what is important to them, if we only listen. By experimenting with a new behavior, I learned the power of listening.

STRUCTURE OF CLASS MEETINGS

Classes met weekly for a full academic year (two semesters) and were three hours in duration. We were seated in a circle and for each class meeting we arranged the chairs in this way. In the first semester, each class had two major components: didactic and experiential. Each was allocated about the same length of time, although at times the didactic preceded the experiential and at other times it was reversed. In the didactic portion of the class, students learned about listening skills and the basic concepts of counseling or interpretive skills. In the experiential part of the class, students practiced the skills that they had learned, or there was a demonstration by the course instructor.

Victoria

I really appreciated the fact that the class was split into didactic and experiential sections. As a visual and hands-on learner, I have often had difficulty comprehending certain theories or approaches because I did not have the opportunity to observe how they are practiced. The in-class demonstrations were probably the most helpful and constructive learning tool for students like me because they truly gave the class a substantiated example of how to apply what has been taught during the instructive portion of the class, as well as throughout their prior psychology courses. In my experience, it is easy to read and hear about counseling – the theoretical approaches and different required skills – but it is not until you witness it first-hand that you truly understand how to conduct an interview with a client. These demonstrations certainly helped me gain the knowledge and confidence to be able to work with clients and, later, conduct interviews on my own.

Sally

Throughout my academic history the desks had been arranged in rows, all facing the instructor at the front of the room. This never failed to instill in me a sense of independence and disinterest, whereby I would busy myself with things unrelated to the course. Sitting in a circle fostered a completely different experience. With classmates on both sides I was compelled to pay close attention to class discussions and get to know my peers; something I had never done previously.

Looking out at the faces of each individual in the classroom, I felt as though I (along with the other students) played a critical part in the lecture. Ami had made it quite clear that he expected each one of us to contribute to the class meeting, as often as possible, and given the seating arrangements it was hard to 'hide' and hope to remain unnoticed. This had a positive effect on both my attendance and participation, which most certainly increased my overall mark in the course. Far more important, however, was the enjoyment factor. I was not just attending a lecture but, rather, participating in a discussion.

Mary

It was the experiential part of the class that kept me coming back for more. Some days we were unleashed to try out a new skill, other days we watched our fellow students role-play a therapeutic encounter. Each class held elements of wonderful unpredictability. Even when we were informed that a guest speaker would be attending a session, we still could not have envisioned the experiential elements of that particular class. One guest speaker that stands out in my mind due to her incredible use of experiential learning was an Expressive Art Therapist. After telling us about the various theories and the healing potential of art therapy, and her particular school of thought, we were given the opportunity to participate in an art therapy session in our classroom. What followed were some of the most intimate and memorable moments of my university years. I watched with reverence as my peers explained their creations; windows into painful pasts, troubled families, fearful futures. The hurt of these young adults, who had, only a few weeks previously, been strangers to me flowed from their hands and onto the classroom wall that we had transformed into a canvas of stories. Neither the Art Therapist, nor Ami, could have taught us instructionally, what we learned that day. Each of us bore witness to the power of creation, the catharsis of molding pain into a piece of art, the healing that could come from purging hurt from our hearts and into our hands. If any of us are ever to become counselors, it is classes such as this one that will help us to remember what heals.

During the second semester, groups of three or four students presented one of the theoretical approaches to counseling that are covered in the textbook to the class, while during the second half of that class meeting, students practiced selected counseling skills that are related to what was presented. The students practiced those skills in groups of three, which would change during the year. The group was composed of a counselor, a client and an observer who was to give both of them feedback at the end of their 30-minute session. These 'demo' counseling sessions quickly become as 'real' as any therapeutic exchange. After 'counseling', the threesome gave and received feedback from their group members, and then we, as a class, discussed it together in an attempt to understand how the 'counselor' promoted openness and comfort for the 'client'.

Victoria
The practice counseling sessions were extremely helpful learning tools that continued throughout the year. They allowed us to take all of the skills that we had been taught and apply them to a practical situation, which helped us better understand their value and significance.

Mary
The classes in which we practiced counseling with each other were both unexpectedly complex and fascinating. Playing the role of the 'counselor' always felt the most challenging for me. Listening, a skill which I thought I was quite adept at proved to be far more difficult especially after I had already been through six or more hours of lectures that day. Attempting to focus my attention fully on my 'client' was a juggling act of simultaneously fighting fatigue, ignoring distractions in the room and my mind, and combating the urge to steer my client toward what I thought she should do. It was in these practice sessions that I first got a feel for how very difficult it is to be a counselor; how incredibly challenging it is, and what an incomparable

gift it can be to make your entire world revolve around another person for an hour.

Course Evaluation

The course evaluation was based on two multiple-choice exams, a class presentation, where all presenters are assumed to contribute equally and thus receive the same grade, and a personal course summary, which provides the students with the opportunity to examine how the material that they learned related to their lives and how it could enrich it and affect their personal growth. Some weight was also given to attendance and participation when calculating the final course grade.

Sally

Hesitantly, I admit, when I first read over the course evaluation I was anything but satisfied. Not only was a portion of my overall grade dependent on participation, I was also being asked to present in front of my peers! Oh sure, this seems like a harsh description of the situation but, at the time, I did not think of it as an over reaction in the least. What if my group partners did not do their fair share of the work? What if I couldn't remember all that I had practiced once I was up there facing the class? What if I let my group down? What if…?

When Ami mentioned the 'assumed equality' of contributed work among group members for the presentations, I was both disappointed and wary. Given that this was a fourth-year class coupled with my aspirations to go to graduate school, the overall grade I attained in the class was very important. I did not favor the prospect of having three other people collaborating on one project with myself. They may end up procrastinating and not contributing anything of value to the group, or perhaps ride on the shirt tails of everyone else in hopes of getting an 'A' without putting forth an effort.

Contrary to ending in ruins, this evaluation scheme worked out very well. Our focus was directed not only to a mark and a topic, though relevant and important, but also on interpersonal development. We, in the presentation group, were dependent on one another for support on our way to reach a common goal. It inspired us to stay on top of the tasks we had assigned between us, meet outside of class frequently, to ensure we were making progress, and it resulted in our attaining a great deal of familiarity with each other. Most importantly, I gained a degree of confidence in trusting and depending on others for an expected outcome in a shared cause, confidence that had eroded as I grew up.

The class presentation consisted of a group of three or four students who presented a theoretical approach of their choosing. They had an hour in which to present the material, involve the class in an exercise, and all the while make the material interesting and captivating.

Sally

Though apprehensive at first, the class presentation was nothing short of a delight. Ami was well aware that some of us were worried about speaking in front of our peers and so he suggested several ideas, one of which helped me tremendously, namely "Before you present inform the class that you are nervous." At first this seemed absurd. However, after an analysis of myself in previous similar situations, something occurred to me: most of my anxiety has centered about attempting to hide my discomfort from others. In this sense, if I could admit that I was nervous before we even began, I would not need to preoccupy myself with trying to act in opposition to how I felt. I adopted the idea and gave it a try. It worked so well that I was actually able to enjoy our presentation. As a group, the three of us had worked hard to make it fun and experiential, both of which we achieved with ease, combining a skit, class activities, and a video clip with humor and exuberance.

Mary

Perhaps what I enjoyed most about this assignment was Ami's disdain for us being exhaustive in our account of the theoretical approach that we were responsible for presenting. Rather than laboriously presenting every nook and cranny of the theory we were responsible for, Ami was more interested in ensuring that we involved the class in our presentation, much as he does when he is teaching. Our goal was to whet the appetites of our fellow classmates, with the hopes that they would further explore the theory themselves. This proved to be a wonderfully interesting way to present, and also meant that those presentations that carefully followed Ami's instructions to be interactive rather than mind-numbingly thorough were very appealing.

The course summary created anxiety and many requests for clarification throughout the year. The assignment was different from almost any assignment that the students were given in their previous three years in undergraduate school. While students are usually asked to write about theoretical issues, and do so as observers and critics, I asked them to actually apply the material to themselves. In other words, if they commented on our first class being somewhat informal and very comfortable, they were asked to reflect on why it was important for them, and what in their life experiences made it unique for them to be introduced in such a way to a group of other students.

Victoria

Although the idea of writing the personal course summary left me feeling quite apprehensive at first, once I had completed it I realized how much I had learned and grown throughout the duration of the course. Since this assignment was so different from any other that I had written before, I was able to gain a great deal of insight, not only into what I had experienced as a result of the class, but also about myself. Furthermore, I feel that this paper required students to consider themselves as well as how and why they are affected by certain things in the same way that a counselor would think about a client. The amount of self-reflection that took place as a result of this assignment, I believe, will make me a better individual, student and counselor. I believe that in order to truly help clients, especially those that are different from oneself, counselors must be aware of themselves, their experiences, and values. This assignment allows students to gain that awareness.

Sally

Upon first discussing the course summary, I found myself to be quite anxious. Though three years in university had resulted in my composing many written assignments and essays, I had never once been given the task of internalizing theories and concepts, and relating their importance to my past experiences. I was perplexed by the very idea of sharing my 'emotional self' with another individual, and doing so on paper. Before this time, I accepted myself as the sum of the events that had colored my life, but this was a very general idea, and one that I had never before explored.

I realized something over the weeks as I thought about the assignment – it was never meant to be easy, nor adhere to a specific design template. How could we expect others to confide in us as therapists when we held back similar thoughts of ourselves? So, throwing fear to the wind, I sat and wrote from the heart. I encouraged (and at times forced) myself to be brutally honest. Despite concerns about how the assignment would be marked, I looked upon the summary as a therapeutic means of personal discovery.

Many of the roads I had traveled down through the course of my life were dark and isolated. The prospect of reliving those memories frightened me, and I can admit it now. There is no doubt that it was emotionally taxing; I felt discomfort, loneliness, even pain, but it was incredibly beneficial in that I came to terms with a past I had long since tried to ignore. A journey is often easier the second time, and looking back I was able to pinpoint characteristics that I wanted to change or strengthen, in order to become a better helper and sensitive friend. It had not occurred to me that moments long past, still affected my day-to-day decisions and behaviors with such strength.

Mary

I am aware that the course summary was a cause for concern to many of my classmates; understandably so, since for three years we had been given assignments to write papers that often merely regurgitated what other theorists thought. Frequently, we were even discouraged from putting our own opinions into our papers. This assignment was different. Terrifying but liberating. Finally, I had been asked to respond to what I was learning with my own thoughts, without mindlessly quoting what other scholars had said before. I was not only permitted, but also required to write a paper riddled with pieces of me. Once again I was reminded that in this class, my story and my thoughts were important. I lined pages with my reactions to our class meetings. Often, there was much pain in my paper, as I wrote of how many classes had triggered my haunting history. But mostly, my course summary was filled with hope. I can honestly say that I have never enjoyed writing a paper more than I did this one. What a gift to be asked to share what went on in my mind as I sat in that class. How wonderful to know that I finally had a professor who wanted to know what I thought.

In the following pages, I describe what takes place in the various class meetings this course entails, the topics we cover, the essence of class activities, the interactions we have, and the exercises in which we engage.

THE FIRST MEETING

It is always jokes that break the ice, so after I ensure that those in attendance are there for a counseling course (and not for a statistics tutorial, for example), I tell a joke to demonstrate that life is a series of struggles and triumphs, just as it is with counseling.

I then devote the rest of the first class to promoting cohesion and student-to-student familiarity. I often share with the students how alienating university campuses may be and how painful it is that students may spend a full academic year together in the same class and even not know each other's names. So, in my classes, I make certain that the situation is very different. I inform the students that we will get to know one another and that I would like them to tell me about their experiences and backgrounds.

Mary

I think that this was the moment I was certain I would like this class. While other professors had acknowledged the vastness of a university campus, and the ease with which students can become lost in the crowd, it was only Ami who seemed to understand how painful this is; the ache that his students feel when they walk amongst a mass of people, unnoticed day after day. I could hear the sadness in his voice as he described this, and his determination that in this class, that would not happen. And he was right. From that first class it was clear to me that each and every one of his students is important to him. He took the time to hear each of our names, and by the end of the first class, he was able to repeat each of them. From our first meeting, we were assured that we were not merely filling in seats, but that each of us has a story, a personality, and a life in which Ami was clearly interested.

I volunteer to be the first one to talk about myself. I share with the students information about my educational 'upbringing', my likes and dislikes, some of my beliefs about education (for instance, that it should be captivating, interesting, and empowering), and I talk about my professional journey since I graduated from university and became a psychologist; the training and postdoctoral posts I have held and the research that I conduct. The students are then free to ask me for clarification of what I shared have with them.

Victoria

I really appreciated the fact that Ami was willing to share information about himself and his life with us. I had never experienced this before, as I was accustomed to having a very limited, if any, relationship with my professors. Him being the first to speak on the very first day of class definitely broke the ice and allowed the rest of us to be more open and comfortable sharing our stories with everyone. Moreover, hearing his professional background was inspiring for many class members since the majority of us were in our final year of study. I think that Ami's story gave us hope for our futures and allowed us to believe that we could accomplish the goals that we had set for ourselves. This in turn, created a sense of optimism and respect among the class, as we knew that our professor was approachable and interested in what we had to say and what we hoped to achieve.

Mary

This part of Ami's class may seem inconsequential; however, Ami's willingness to self-disclose some of his story set the stage for each of us to feel comfortable to do the same. Furthermore, being allowed a glimpse of Ami as more than a professor, with a past of challenges and a future of dreams, was fascinating. Suddenly, this man, my superior and evaluator, had become a tangible human being.

I then ask the students to spend several minutes speaking with the student who sits to their right. Four to five minutes later, they are asked to repeat the process with the person who is sitting to their left. Afterwards, I instruct the students to speak with a classmate who may be sitting on the other side of the room and be prepared to tell their classmates about that person later.

Victoria

Following the first class I found myself to be in a state of utter amazement. In my three years at university I had never encountered an experience like this where the professor was so intent on everyone in the class knowing one another and feeling comfortable with one another. I was not sure why it was so important then, but looking back I can now understand that without that initial 'interview process' we would not have felt comfortable enough with one another to share some of the things that we have shared over the course of the year. Although we did not cover any course material in our first class meeting, we did something more important; we formed relationships with one another and secured a comfort level within the class and with the professor that would shape the rest of the year and the course. The first session allowed the class, as a whole, to create rules for everyone to abide by and agreements with one another that facilitated open communication. One of my biggest obstacles throughout my university career has been my usual hesitation and reluctance to speak in class. However, I was able to overcome my anxieties as a result of the comfortable, accepting atmosphere that was created on the first day of the class, and maintained throughout the duration of the course.

Sally

University is supposed to prepare you for the world outside. We each sit in classrooms and listen to various professors lecture about topics we hope will be useful at some point in our careers. We do our best to learn the facts and figures that are part of our assigned readings, and try to apply that knowledge when we take a test. However, university often fails to teach us about something that is critical to both our day-to-day lives, and our future vocational activities – person-to-person interaction.

In this particular instance, introducing ourselves to other members of the classroom served as the framework to building a 'team-atmosphere'. After sharing a bit about ourselves with the rest of the class, and hearing about the experiences of others, we immediately felt as though we were part of a collective whole. More importantly, this gave us practical experience of introducing ourselves to new individuals, while encouraging others to feel open enough to share similar information.

Had someone asked my opinion on setting aside half of an entire lecture for introductions, before attending this course, I would have confidently said it was a colossal waste of valuable time. I would not have foreseen any benefits outside of maybe breaking the ice on the first day of a new academic year, and even this I would have thought to be short lived. Surely time could be better spent on course material. Yet, opinions do change.

These brief introductions served as stepping-stones, leading us from individual units (persons) who first entered the class towards a gestalt or cohesive group. Even by communicating the most trivial of facts about myself I immediately felt as though I belonged, and was part of something bigger than myself. While each person in the class was speaking, I was trying to remember names and small details about them. Even when the second class rolled around, it was evident that people felt comfortable with their surroundings and many of us smiled at each other in recognition. Though at the time I had no idea what to expect of the course, in hindsight I can say without hesitation that this was an important factor in building confidence and security within the classroom.

Mary

I remember this part of the first class well. I remember the awkwardness of speaking to the strangers in my class, something I had rarely done in all my years as a university student. I remember the sounds of chairs being pulled back as my classmates hesitantly stood. And today, nearly a year later, I can still remember each of the students I spoke with in that first class. I'm sure that Ami could see his students changing as the year progressed, but it was this activity of getting to know a few classmates that helped me to see just how much of an effect this course had on some of us. One girl with whom I spoke was finishing her psychology degree with the intention of heading into dentistry. However, by the end of the year, she had been accepted into a very prestigious graduate school to continue her education in psychology instead. I can only imagine how instrumental this course had been in her decision to alter her career path.

That first interaction with my fellow classmates began a year of intimate disclosures and was the start of many friendships. Those first students I spoke with became the ones I sat next to for many of the classes to come. They became the ones who connected with me at the start of each class, reminding me that in that room, I was not just another stranger, but a person with a name and a story. And very soon after that first class, these students were no longer strangers to me either.

The class is then seated in a circle and each person tells us about the last classmate with whom they spoke. While listening, I attempt to connect 'the name to the face'. When the students are done presenting each other, I am then able to go around the room and repeat all of their names. The students are quite touched to see that I have taken the time and made the effort to remember their names. Throughout the year, I ask them to refresh my memory of their name, but before long, their names are safely deposited in my long-term memory.

Sally
When Ami began to recite each of our names after listening to us speak, I could not help but break out in a grin and applaud along with many other students. It was not his grandiose display of short-term memory that had impressed me, rather, that he desired to know each and every one of us on a first-name basis. No longer just another 'nine digit number', I immediately felt as though I was an important member of the class and was motivated to participate throughout the year.

Up until this point, at almost 90 minutes into the first class, we have not yet discussed the course at all; not the subject matter, nor what the students would be expected to know, nor what requirements they would need to fulfill in order to pass the course. After all of the students are relaxed and feel less alienated than they usually do in new classes, we talk about how to successfully pass this course, and the students are given a seven-page, very detailed course description. They can then ask questions and their concerns are addressed.

There are two more things that are left to cover before our first meeting came to a close. First was the agreement that students were asked to sign, which informed them that the personal material that they would choose to disclose in class required that they promise that they would not discuss with anyone, in or out of the class, confidential information that was shared with them in class. Students almost unanimously liked that agreement, signing up it willingly and sharing with me their delight at the fact that they are assured of, and encouraged, to maintain confidentiality. Over the years, as far as I know, this confidentiality was never compromised and the agreement fostered openness and sharing in the class.

Sally

After signing the confidentiality agreement and exiting our first class, there were audible comments regarding the ineffectiveness of such a contract in combination with questions as to why it was necessary. Being the budding clinical psychologist I was, I looked at the agreement with awe and promised myself I would adhere to it. Even so, I was skeptical if other students in the class would do the same. In fact, I was so curious over the matter that towards the end of the year I started asking people about it. I was astonished when each of the students I talked with stated that they had not compromised the agreement and were proud of this.

I, as well, was pleased that I had not discussed information that had transpired during the course outside of the classroom. A point of paramount significance for me, however, was the effect this had on my ability to share aspects of myself with the class. Under the aegis of the agreement, and in combination with the connection I felt with my classmates and the professor, I was able to disclose material about myself that I had guarded fiercely beforehand. And having done so, I was able to generalize this behavior to other aspects of my life, serving to fortify many continuing relationships and foster the commencement of several others.

The confidentiality agreement inspired growth by helping people to be open and share in a safe environment. Discussing personal and emotional experiences can be difficult with those you are closest to, let alone with peers whom you know you will have to sit face to face with, every week, until the end of the academic year. It is an easier feat when you trust that whatever you might say will stay with those in the classroom and not be discussed without you present.

Having said this, it is important to note that upholding the agreement was much harder than I had first imagined. I found several of the classes to be so interesting that I had to consciously refrain from sharing my experiences with friends. Over the years it becomes second nature for us to talk about our day with those we love and trust. By not compromising the confidentiality agreement that we signed in this counseling course, those of us who have decided to pursue careers in various fields of therapy received valuable experience towards upholding similar agreements that will be shared with our future clients.

The first class meeting ends with a short assignment that is given to the students. Each is asked to answer, and bring to class the following week, their answers to a list of eight questions. They are meant to give me a better understanding of who the students are, what their goals are in taking the class (beyond, of course, their need to fulfill their program's requirements and their hopes of getting an 'A'), what their expectations of the professor and their fellow students are, and how we can create the most conducive atmosphere for them to learn and benefit from the material. In the following weeks, once I receive their answers to the eight questions, I share with the students the highlights of what they wrote and we further discuss ways to achieve their goals.

Just before we end our first class, I share with the students my philosophical approach to counseling and provide them with a roadmap of the course and the topics that we will cover. After having experienced three years filled with theoretical courses detailing conceptual theories and approaches, when students attend a counseling course, they expect action! They are in their fourth year of university, feel that they have learned all they need to, and are enthusiastic to be given and taught skills that they can utilize when offering counseling, helping people, and contributing to others' mental health. I felt the same in my last year of undergraduate studies and in graduate school as well.

Mary

Once again, Ami understands his students well. By fourth year, I was almost exploding with a desire 'to do'. It would have been torture to sit in a counseling class, one that takes so much of what I had learned so far, and have been asked to sit passively while concepts were once again dictated to me. Instead, our classes were taught without PowerPoint slides or endless lectures. Rather than furiously scribbling down definitions and theories as our professor monopolized the podium, our class was alive with discussions. While Ami frequently noted what several prominent counselors believed were the skills necessary to be a successful counselor, he more often asked us to describe what we felt would make an effective counselor. Classes were structured in a way that would allow us to actively utilize what we were taught. And for me, as well as for many of my peers, what we learned in this class reached far beyond the confines of our classroom. I learned listening skills that I eagerly put into practice in my everyday interactions. I tapped into the power of empathy with my friends and family, especially when there seemed to be nothing else I could do to ease their pain. I learned the healing potential of making a person feel that they are valued. And I watched in awe as many of my relationships changed because of this class.

It may be that the roadmap of the course is a temporary disappointment for some. Here is the reason: I share with the students my belief that the most important therapeutic ingredient is the client–therapist relationship. It is less important, I add, what school of thought, technological advances, or techniques the therapist may have in their 'toolkit', since whatever approach they use may be helpful to the client in the context of a good, caring, and empowering therapeutic relationship. Consequently, the students are told that we will spend the whole first semester (half of the academic year) on understanding and learning how to develop proper therapeutic relationships. The students often look amazed, but seemed ready for the journey.

Sally

Thinking back to the first class, I can humorously recall some of the faces of students seated around me when the professor announced that half of the year would be dedicated to talking about one specific topic: the therapeutic relationship. It was safe to assume that I was not the only person who was a little shocked. Granted, I was concerned that there would not be enough time remaining to cover the rest of the items noted in the syllabus but I was excited nonetheless. My thoughts at the time: anything that merits an entire semester of discussion must be critical to all persons entering a helping profession.

The various counseling techniques are covered in the second semester. The first class then ends with a definition of counseling and psychotherapy, and by reviewing the different professionals who offer therapy (i.e., psychologists, psychiatrists, social workers, the clergy, family physicians, etc.) and how their approaches differ.

EVERY DYSFUNCTION IS FUNCTIONAL

This is one of the first examples of reframing that I gave to my class. Whilst people in general may stigmatize or at least scoff at emotional troubles or psychiatric disturbances, I provide the class with an explanation that views those dysfunctions from an evolutionary perspective. I share with the class the understanding that all of us *can* cope. However, we do so in various ways. When we can no longer cope in a healthy way, we resort to neurotic behavior, and those whose ego strength is not able to withstand even that may resort to psychotic behavior. However, whether neurotic or psychotic, the behavior that, on the face of it, could be referred to as a disturbance or dysfunction is usually helpful and protective of us. The most interesting fact about such dysfunctions is their functionality.

For example, I discuss with the students the psychological mechanisms of a 'writer's cramp', where a perfectly healthy hand starts to shake uncontrollably at the person's attempts to write. Alternatively, I discuss a case that I treated many years ago of a bright woman in her 20s who was an only child and asked for my help in order to deal with her agoraphobia. Her condition had deteriorated steadily until she was unable to go to work and was mostly housebound. Previous attempts at treatment had not helped, she claimed. Believing that her agoraphobia was actually helpful to her in some way, we explored her childhood, family dynamics, and her relationship with her parents.

Being an only child, her parents planned for her to go to university and be the 'brain of the family'. Having had low self-esteem and a great fear of disappointing her loving parents, she was terrified of university. Being unable to quash her parents' dreams by either refusing to attend university or attending it and failing, she developed a panic attack on her first bus trip to school. That afforded her a 'convenient' and acceptable excuse for avoiding attending university, and since her phobia was so functional and helpful, she 'hung on to it' until our treatment (addressing the underlying issues) freed her of her need for it and so helped her confront her parents and become free of her phobia.

This story often has quite a significant effect on the class. 'Wheels begin turning' in the students' minds, insight is reported, and great interest in the course is generated.

Sally

'Every dysfunction is functional'. Admittedly, I liked the way this sounded, but it wasn't until I heard the story of Ami's patient that I truly understood how well the phrase encapsulated the essence of a dysfunction. Intuitively it made sense; people do not wake up early one morning and decide, "Today is a good day to become agoraphobic." However, it takes a concrete example to solidify an idea that may not be fully understood.

Mary

'Every dysfunction is functional'. It can be the reason that the battered woman does not leave her abuser. It can help to explain why the young boy with obsessive–compulsive disorder washes his hands for the 37th time that day. It is why I could not go near a parking lot for years.

When I was in my last year of high school, I was in a terrifying accident as a pedestrian. A truck hit me and then the driver, not feeling the impact or seeing me lying behind his vehicle, proceeded to drive over my foot. Though I earnestly attempted to deny its impact, this experience shook me and tore away any teenage beliefs of invincibility. I was acutely aware that had I fallen just slightly to the right, it would have been my back that would have been shattered, instead of my foot. Still, I refused to consciously indulge in any of my fears, refusing to even use crutches, so as not to draw attention to myself. I wanted desperately to forget that this event had ever happened. Shortly after the accident, I began to have panic attacks whenever I saw the rear end of a truck. This fear slowly began to encompass all vehicles, and before long, I could not walk through parking lots, or any other place where I could encounter the back of a vehicle. I took great pains to walk around the front of cars, and to avoid any place that might cause me to fall into a panic. My phobia affected my life and was difficult to disguise from others. Perhaps even more painful than the fear itself was the judgment of my friends who saw my fears as irrational and trivial. But my fear of taillights served me well for a few years. I was able to see the faces of drivers and anticipate their actions. My phobia, though incapacitating in many ways, also made it possible for me to feel as though I could make my world safer.

Knowing that behaviors, ones which appear to have no value in their limitations, actually exist because they serve a purpose, can be the key to understanding another human being's distress. A counselor who is aware that a client, who seems resistant to treatment, is not simply another case of non-compliance, but is actually using a dysfunctional behavior in order to function in his world, can feel empathy for her client when no one else can. The moment that I was taught to search for the sanity in seemingly 'insane' actions, my desire to judge both myself and other people fell to the wayside.

THE REST OF THE SEMESTER

From the second class on we are engaged in covering the following topics:

- A) A quick review of abnormal psychology, and an overview of how treating the mentally ill has developed since the Middle Ages.
- B) The different specialty areas in counseling and some of the characteristics that students need to develop in order to find those areas interesting and fulfilling for them.

C) The characteristics of a counselor. This topic has two full classes devoted to it, and includes:

1. The various characteristics and behaviors that therapists display, regardless of their theoretical orientation, are discussed and illustrated. An exercise aimed at illustrating those characteristics then follows. The students discuss the characteristics of a counselor, teacher, or someone else from the healthcare profession, which in their experience proved to be helpful. This then personalizes those characteristics that are important and that they may need to acquire.
2. The personal characteristics, interests, and values that those who are considering entering the field of counseling would need in order to succeed.

Sally

This experiential activity was twofold in its beneficial effect on the class. For starters it forced us to actively search out the characteristics that we have found to be effective in our pasts. By composing this list from personal experience rather than memorizing something from a text, we were better able to both remember and conceptualize the material. It also allowed us to compare ourselves against this list, giving us some indication as to behaviors we may need to strengthen or even obtain. I found this to be of utmost importance. These characteristics and behaviors we exhibit are things that cannot be modified simply by reading a book. They may need to be worked on for a long period of time, with much practice and patience. Just because we, as students, retain facts, figures, theories and techniques rather well does not mean that we necessarily internalize the material. A perfect example of this would be the ability to listen. We learn in this class that this is important in therapy and we nod our heads in agreement; "Of course it is!" However, this knowledge does not guarantee that we, ourselves, are good listeners. Only when we observe ourselves and compare our behaviors to others can we be clear on how we operate. This activity helped us do just that: open our eyes to several things we may want to work towards changing in order to be better counselors (and all round people).

D) One of the central sections of the course is the therapeutic relationship. Several classes are devoted to it, and they cover the following:

1. Why is the therapeutic relationship important and what makes it good? During a class exercise, the students are asked to reflect on relationships that they may have had with physicians, counselors, teachers, or friends, and to identify what made those relationships helpful. This makes concrete and brings to life the more esoteric elements of the discussion on relationships in therapy.
2. What makes the therapeutic relationship 'therapeutic'? Here, the discussion focuses on client-centered therapy and its major tenets, Langs' (1972, 1988) bi-personal field, Cory's (1996) pillars of counseling, and Kottler's (2004) textbook, which are reviewed as an example of what helpful therapeutic relationships should include.
3. The commonalities and the differences between friendship and the client–therapist relationship are reviewed.
4. Transference and counter-transference – their influence on therapy and on everyday life. Why they are beneficial and how addressing them can benefit the therapeutic relationship is discussed.
5. Sexual tension and how to address it if it occurs during counseling. The possibility that sexual tension may be present when two adults meet regularly and have an intimately (albeit one-sided) close relationship is discussed as either a normal occurrence or as transference or counter-transference.

Sally

Glancing at the clock as he pulls into his usual parking spot, he is pleased to see that ten minutes remain before today's much-anticipated meeting. He saunters up the steps to the building, through the doors and towards the elevators that will carry him to her floor. Unnoticed, he runs his hand through his hair as he thinks back over the last couple of months. From the first moment they met, she had been different from all the other women in his life. With a warm smile she focused all of her attention on him, listening when he spoke, and never passing judgment. Since meeting her, even his coworkers have noticed the change in his confidence and mood. He was a happy man. Knocking lightly, he adjusts his shirt before strolling into his therapist's office.

Given the ideal circumstances with which a client becomes acquainted with his therapist, it is not terribly unreasonable that he may come to exhibit an attraction for her. After all, she is an individual who never loses her temper while showing unconditional patience and kindness when he is most in need of support.

As plausible as this may be, I had never given much thought to the subject of sexual tension. In fact, I had not thought of it at all. None of the textbooks I had read had addressed this, and no professor had mentioned it. It is only through this discussion that many of us in the class even became aware of such intricacies that counseling sessions may include.

THE THERAPEUTIC RELATIONSHIP

To enter the Path of Psychotherapy is to begin together a special relationship. In this relationship, I will do my best to understand who you are ... I will not tell you what to do. I cannot make you grow or do your growing for you. I will help you to become more aware, more loving, more able to fashion a richer, fuller life for which you accept responsibility. On the path of psychotherapy, pain will be part of the experience we share. I will help you face it, accept it, and use it to grow...

Welch, 1998; p. 155–156

As I mentioned previously, the therapeutic relationship is the cornerstone of psychotherapy. Regardless of the therapeutic approach that one uses, a good therapeutic relationship is the foundation of therapy. Although the students are often in a 'rush' to learn how to actually do therapy, I share with them the view that one cannot write words, or develop it into a story, if one does not first learn the alphabet (see also Rokach, 1986).

I ask students what they think psychotherapy is and, usually, the regular answers of, "It is meant to help," "It offers people hope," or "It corrects their thinking/feelings" come up.

An Attention Focuser

The students are asked to reflect on the various relationships that they have had in their lives, and describe a relationship that had a positive effect on them, and one that had a negative effect. They are then asked to explain what made that relationship so influential. The students, with some guidance from me, compose a list that eventually lists the dos and don'ts of a good therapeutic relationship.

Amongst the features that we cover and discuss are:

1. True caring, a non-judgmental attitude and respect towards the client, whoever he or she is.
2. A good therapeutic relationship is one that promotes comfortable openness, confidentiality (with limitations as prescribed by law and by the governing professional body), and keeping in mind at all times that the client is the important one in the relationship, and all that transpires in the therapeutic hour is geared towards helping him or her.
3. Instilling hope, reassurance and empowering the client such that, if done in the appropriate time and manner, the therapy can be invaluable in helping them.
4. Langs (1972) highlighted the bidirectional nature of the therapeutic relationship and the mutual influence that the client and therapist have on each other. We highlight these features, including transference, counter-transference, and sexual attraction, and explain how they can occur in a caring, intimate, and open relationship, such as a good therapeutic relationship, and how to address them.

Mary

I had been taught in previous psychology courses that the effectiveness of therapy is not to be found in the type of therapy used, but in the fostering of the therapeutic relationship. What I had not been taught was how to create this incredibly healing relationship. And yet now, as I look back on our class, I see that Ami did more than merely attempt to teach us how to craft such a relationship. He moved beyond providing us with tools and techniques, and instead, structured the entire course as an example of a therapeutic relationship, with professor acting as 'counselor', and students as 'clients'. True to his word, Ami devoted the first semester to developing a therapeutic alliance with his students. In our first class he behaved much as he would with a client, telling us what to expect from him and this course, explaining the limits of confidentiality, and revealing a bit about himself to foster trust and openness. As classes continued, he frequently encouraged our own self-exploration and healing, while carefully maintaining structure and emotional safety.

5. The pressure to 'do something' and 'curling'.

One of the most 'damaging' aspects of learning how to effectively help others is the pressure that is felt to intervene, direct, or actively steer the client in a specific or 'better' direction. It takes some discussion and honesty on the part of the students to admit that when such pressure was felt by them (and it is invariably felt by newcomers to the counseling profession), it was for their own benefit, so that they felt that they were doing 'something' for the client, were helping the client, and were being 'good' counselors.

Sally

This is something I had not noticed even though I was guilty of it. I started the class without conscious awareness of my desire to lead those people who were confiding in me down some more beneficial path in life, at least from my own perspective. By doing so I almost felt satisfied; they were given direction and a new outlook on the problem, which led me to believe I had done a good job. It took adjustment, self-awareness and practice, on my part, to keep my mouth shut – and listen!

We discuss the need to learn the 'art' of listening. Being with and for the client and listening to what the client says, what is not said, and attending to his or her body language. Only through listening can the counselor truly understand the client and where they are at.

Sally

When a patient goes to the physician complaining of a stomachache, the doctor has a couple of choices. He can tell the patient that a flu is going around and to wait it out. He might prescribe medication to alleviate the pain. Or, he may take what some would argue is the correct path of action and dig deeper, so as to use all the information available to him to make a correct diagnosis.

In therapy, similar actions are required. We have to listen to what the patient is telling us, determine what they're not telling us, and observe how they are acting. Only then can we try to resolve the hidden problem instead of simply treating an observable symptom. We discussed, as a group, how some clients wear masks that they may be unable to remove without assistance from a counselor, within the context of a warm therapeutic alliance. Even though they actively seek help it does not ensure that they will come to therapy without the defenses that keep them safe.

Curling is the game where a person pushes a round marble stone on a smooth surface, and two 'helpers' quickly brush the surface with brooms, so that the stone can reach its target. I see the client as the stone, and the therapist as merely the broom that helps the stone get to where it needs to go. The best thing that the therapist can do for and with the client is to understand them and then share that understanding with the client, and when appropriate, design a specific treatment program. Understanding the client can come only by attentive, active listening.

Class Exercises

The class repeatedly engages in counseling sessions in which they take turns being the listener (i.e., counselor). They are often amazed to discover:

> A) How difficult listening is, and
> B) How beneficial to understanding the client listening truly is.

Sally

My first time as 'counselor' in our sessions left me surprised by the deceptively hard task of listening. I thought it would be easy; after all, I had been doing just that for decades (hadn't I?!). But once I started to observe myself, I noticed it was exceedingly difficult to listen without interjecting my own preconceived notion of how she 'should' have been responding to my questions and even how she should behave in social interactions! I felt compelled to discuss the matter at hand rather than encouraging her to speak freely.

This exercise helped me to realize something important about myself that I might not have noticed otherwise: an ever-present belief that in order to help, I must actively 'do' something so as to direct the person along a 'better' path. Simply listening had made me uncomfortable, and I felt almost as though I was being lazy on the job (role-playing a counselor). Nevertheless, this discomfort gradually dwindled and with practice I began to see just how beneficial listening is for the client. Not only was I able to retain more of the information that was being relayed to me, the other students who were my clients became visibly more relaxed and attested to this during discussion.

One of the differences between a good friendship and a good therapeutic relationship is that while we commonly want to nurture a satisfying friendship and hope that it will last for a long time, the therapeutic relationship's explicit goal is to end as soon as therapeutically possible. The therapeutic relationship exists for the client's benefit, and while the relationship may become intimate, bi-directionally nurturing, pleasant, fulfilling, helpful, and affirming for the therapist as well as the client, its goal is to end – to stop once the client can deal with life's issues, or cope on their own.

Mary

I think that this point illustrates one of the most difficult aspects of therapy for both the client and the counselor. Humans seek connection with others. We do this sometimes at the expense of other necessities. We search for ways to create relationships with others, even though we risk being hurt. We do this because we have to. Research does not argue this point. We cannot thrive without human contact. From the moment we are born, we seek to be held. As children we learn to create friendships with others that often follow us for many years. As adults, the desire to surround ourselves with enduring relationships is a strong motivator in much of our interactions with others.

The therapeutic relationship does not allow us to indulge in this deep and powerful desire to create long-term relationships. In fact, a therapeutic alliance that does not have the conclusion of the relationship as one of its specific goals exists for reasons other than to aid the client.

The very nature of the counseling relationship makes termination even more unnatural. Clients divulge extremely intimate and private details of their lives. Counselors are privy to secrets that may never have been uttered to friends or even lovers. This sharing can create a fierce bond, one which both client and counselor may not wish to end. But end it they must. One of the best indicators of a successful therapeutic relationship is the ability for the client to reach a point in which she can move on without her counselor.

It is perhaps for this reason that counseling can be considered a very lonely profession. Moments of profound connection with clients are often overshadowed by the certainty that this relationship will one day come to a close.

Loneliness

That is a 'biggy' in most clients' lives, not necessarily only because they are alone and isolated, but also because they may have many mental health problems or feel misunderstood, unaccepted, or even rejected. In my experience as a psychologist of 30 years, I have heard of loneliness from each and every client, although this is not often the presenting problem. Consequently, one of the most important things for a therapist to do is to ensure that their client feels supported, accepted, validated, and truly cared for.

Often, a good and open therapeutic alliance may account for most of the positive changes that the client may experience. I share with the class my research on loneliness, its main features, and how it can 'play out in clients' lives, and all of students can relate to this. I relate some of my own loneliness experiences, and those of my clients and their improvement in light of a close, caring, and empowering therapeutic alliance (see Rokach, 2007; 2011).

Sally

It was this topic, above all the rest, which led me to understand, beyond question, the importance of establishing a good therapeutic relationship. I can now appreciate how this loving and supportive therapeutic environment, even by itself, can often lead to improvement for many persons. Previous to this lecture I had accepted the power of such an alliance but could not concretely internalize the benefits. However, looking back, I can determine the characteristics of the people who helped me overcome bouts of loneliness, those of acceptance, love, and understanding; key features in a good rapport between therapist and client. This was the link I was in need of in order to personalize the material. I had not seen the parallels between others and myself.

In a society where isolation and dysfunction are frowned upon, even though they are encouraged by the very same society, we often try to hide from the world (and ourselves) those experiences that are seen as negative. During this class, I relived those moments in my life when I felt completely alone, and in doing so, intimately understood how a loving and open relationship with another person can make a world of positive change.

Mary

I do not find it hard to believe that Ami has uncovered loneliness in the hearts of each of his clients. And it does not surprise me that this is not usually the presenting concern. In our society, loneliness is experienced with shame. Admitting that we are lonely is often met with pity or judgment. Most people do not want to have others feeling sorry for them. But even worse can be the underlying accusation in the question, "Why are you lonely?", as though it might be due to some fault of our own, something that we could easily change.

Loneliness manifests itself in so many ways that it is easily overlooked. Our society so swiftly hides loneliness with labels of broken-heartedness, anger, sadness, and grief. It took me many years to understand that my experiences with depression are both rooted and covered in loneliness. It is loneliness that began my depression in the first place, and perpetuates it even now. And yet, I never approached a therapist with loneliness as a concern.

There is an irony in the fact that we all experience loneliness. Many times I have walked alone in a crowd; drowning in loneliness and wondering how many of the people I am passing are feeling the same isolation. I often wonder what it is that keeps us from reaching out to the people around us. This feeling was intensified for me in the surroundings of my university. Navigating through a campus cluttered with strangers, often remaining nameless and faceless to other students even as I entered classrooms, was painful. But Ami's class was a welcome, though at first an unsettling change. Not only were the students' of his class part of an environment that encouraged us to reach out to each other, but we also broke the social silence and spoke openly and candidly about our experiences of loneliness.

The therapist who is keenly aware of the rampant loneliness in his clients can understand just how healing the establishment of a therapeutic relationship is. Similarly, the professor who is not only aware of the loneliness in his students, but is responsive to this, is in the position to create a classroom experience that attempts to break this pattern of alienation, and becomes part of the healing process. The alliance found between client and counselor, and between professor and student has the potential to drive much deeper than our dominant and superficial means of daily communication. These relationships are built on the deep desire to know someone else. It was clear from the start of Ami's class that his intention was not only to come to know us better himself, but to teach us to seek to know our fellow students as well. What better cure for loneliness than to encounter a person who takes the time, effort, and sincere interest to understand our own story.

THE FIRST IN-CLASS COUNSELING SESSION

An article that I wrote (Rokach, 1986) clearly delineates the hesitant and questioning first meeting that the therapist has with the client. The students are asked to read their textbook's relevant chapter and other material, and then reflect on how they would feel during the first session: a) as a therapist, and b) as a client. Students who are themselves clients are asked to share how they felt when attending their own first therapeutic session, and how they gathered information about the therapist and his approach. The students were then asked to reflect on how they would feel in the role of a therapist approaching their first session with a client. Invariably, they mention their anxieties, self-doubt, and insecurities about being a counselor, and a class discussion ensues. Making it personal results in a lively discussion.

Sally

Trying to imagine how I would feel as a therapist going into my first session left me nervous. I would not know how to act, might forget important points of inquiry, and even fail to positively affect the client or build the foundations of a good rapport. Granted, these worries were warranted as I had never been in such a position, but this mental activity left my mind heavy with questions. The class discussion that ensued did much to alleviate my worry. My anxiety was justified and many of my concerns were mirrored in the questions asked by other students.

It is now time to demonstrate an initial therapy session to the class. Weeks ahead of this time, I check with one or two students whether they would agree to participate in a counseling demonstration (to which they also volunteer at the beginning of the year), and a student is then chosen. The class is seated in a circle around the student and myself, as we both sit facing each other in the middle. I ask the class to remain quiet and write down their impressions and questions. They are reminded of their promise to keep class discussions confidential. The client/student is:

1. Told to ignore her peers and it is suggested to the student that, within 2–3 minutes, they will be so engrossed in the session that they will oblivious to their surroundings.
2. The student is asked to describe their feelings at the moment. Usually, these consist of anxiety, embarrassment, and uncertainty of what the session will include.
3. The student is asked to help me get to know them, and to speak only about those topics and issues that they are comfortable discussing. The student is told that at no point will any pressure be put on them whatsoever to discuss what they may not be ready to discuss.

Very quickly thereafter, the student openly talks about the current issues that are troubling them, and after about 40 minutes, we end the session with a debriefing of the student/client and of the class. Witnessing an initial session is truly beneficial for demonstrating the points that we have previously mentioned about the therapeutic relationship. After the session is over, I ask the student to relate how they feel, any comments or questions they have are welcomed, and we then 'face' the class together for a discussion of what ensued. In subsequent classes, we repeat the demonstration with different students each time.

Sally

Class demonstrations of this form were of paramount importance in clarifying the topics we had discussed in the class. Not only did they serve as a visual aid, but also they completely transformed our beliefs and ideas.

Hesitantly, I admit that I was not expecting much from this 'first session' for a couple of reasons: the client was a student who was, like the rest of us, familiar with the professor plus she was surrounded by her peers. Much to my surprise, these things did not seem to have a noticeable impact! In a matter of minutes, with the help of Ami, she was discussing very personal matters of the heart and completely disregarding the rest of the class. I found it quite amazing how comfortable she felt talking with him, especially in such an environment.

This demonstration gave us a very real idea about what to expect during our first sessions as therapists. We were able to listen to what Ami said, as well as watch how he interacted with her beyond words: eye contact, body language, and facial expressions. We were then able to ask questions and even critique what had occurred, which served to solidify what we had learned throughout the class as well as dismantling some of the incorrect assumptions we had held about therapist interaction with the client and the first session.

Mary

After taking Ami's course for a little less than a month, I volunteered to participate in an in-class counseling session with him. In my course summary, I tried to capture this memorable experience: "He sat facing me, eyes intent and waiting. I could feel the classroom huddled in anticipated silence, waiting for us to start. What had I gotten myself into? I made sure to wear a thick sweater to school that day, just in case I needed something to hide behind. What would I say? What would we talk about?

"And then it happened. Ami and I entered into something that only we could be a part of. The twenty-five pairs of eyes staring at us melted into the background, just as he had said they would. I really had not trusted him until we began. I really don't trust anyone. But in those moments, in that session, I trusted Ami. I trusted him not to judge me. And more than that, I trusted that he was interested in me. Not in who I wanted him to think I was, but who I really am beyond the walls I so carefully place around me. He paid attention to me. The minutes slipped by unnoticed as he asked me to tell him about my music, my writing, and my family. He actually thought I was interesting – that my life was worth noting, even the details that I had been taught to ignore by every other therapist I had met along my search for healing. I remember relief at the ease of our conversation. I remember shock at how wonderful it felt to speak so freely about my life. And I remember aching. I wanted to tell him so much more. I wanted him to know the stories I couldn't tell. I tested him repeatedly; I watched his eyes for disapproval. I noted his posture for signs of boredom. I waited for him to steer me in the direction he thought we should go, and when he did not lead, I melted with relief at being given control and safety. And so I wanted to tell him more. While I spoke of the man who had hurt me repeatedly for three years, I longed to tell him of the ones in between who had stolen every last piece of my purity. While he listened to me talk of a relationship full of distance and alienation, I thought of how easy it would be to tell him of the babies I had carried but never held. So much respect. So much empathy. So much accomplished in one session that could not be done with the years of therapy I had previously experienced.

"I had held back, but only because somewhere in my mind I knew that we were not alone. I answered the questions that came from my classmates, but wondered what questions they were refraining from asking. I could see acceptance and understanding in their eyes, but they had not heard the whole story. What would they think of me if they knew it all? I did not trust them, though I wanted to. But for some reason, I trusted this man who sat beside me telling me how courageous I had been for sharing some pieces of my story. Did he know there was more? Does he know how those moments changed me? What had I gotten myself into? I knew now: I had opened the door to my healing. And I will never be able to shut it again. I had allowed myself to hope for one hour. And for one hour, I remembered what it was like to trust again.

***

"Robert Langs speaks of the importance of approaching each session with a client "without memory" (Langs, 1972). Rather than believing that we understand a client and have him/her figured out, Langs suggests that counselors err on the side of humility. In order for the therapist to be open to going wherever the client needs to go, the therapist must not assume to know the client's needs or anticipate the client's responses. It is a common theme in our class that Ami reminds us that people will always talk about what they really need to talk about, if we only just let them. In his session with me, I never had the sense of struggling with him over what we should be discussing. Nothing was deemed to be unimportant. No detail was too small. Not for a second did I feel apologetic for leading the conversation to new areas. In my previous encounters with therapy, I have always felt that I lacked the discipline to stay on topic. If I had decided to attend counseling because I wanted to work on my relationship with my boyfriend, any musings about my childhood or my relationships with other significant people in my life were brushed aside as extraneous and trifle material. My therapists always carried an agenda of which I was acutely aware. And they always seemed to have decided that they knew what I was going to say or do – that they had me figured out. This pattern in my therapeutic relationships left me trapped within the confines of who I thought my therapist thought I was. I never felt that I could surprise them, and I was always fighting the fear that I was boring them or worse, so predictable that my problems were insignificant and could be easily resolved if I would just stop being my predictable self.

"My session with Ami embodied the concepts of Carl Rogers' client-centered counseling effortlessly. Kottler and Shepard (2008) note that this approach is "more a 'way of being' with the client than it is a 'way of doing'" (p. 134). I truly felt that Ami had spent the hour with me trying to enter my world. Rather than using several specific techniques to draw me out, he did not appear to be working on anything but really trying to understand me. His mastery of empathy and refrain from judgment seemed to spread throughout our classroom. His practice of being quick to encourage me and slow to critique me have become increasingly emulated by my classmates as well. I see now the weight of importance of the therapeutic relationship. Once established, it becomes the basis of safety and respect that is so important for instigating change."

CONCLUSION

Although this appendix does not include a quantified analysis of my students' personal growth, their learning, and the changing of the myths they may have held about counseling, their written course-and-instructor evaluations provide ample evidence that these goals were achieved. Students repeatedly reported that not only were they able to apply the counseling techniques and concepts to their own issues and conflicts, but they had also enhanced their armamentarium of introspection and reflection, interpersonal skills, and gained a deeper understanding of themselves and others. The course thus demonstrates that personal growth and learning can occur in interesting, fun, and creative ways. Obviously, the instructor, along with the students, plays an important role in facilitating and creating a safe environment where risk taking, vulnerability, and openness can occur.

Sally

From the very first class there was an established sense of intimacy and openness between the class members. We talked about ourselves, began to learn each other's names, and signed a confidentiality agreement that offered security and encouragement to voice our opinions and experiences. Throughout my educational journey I hesitantly admit that I was frequently absent from lectures, and on the occasions I did attend, rarely felt the impulse or need to pay attention. This class was different. My attendance was almost perfect, I looked forward to each lecture, and the sense of empowerment instilled throughout the semester made it possible for me to actually speak out in front of my peers – something I had never before attempted.

Here I was, sitting in the classroom, anxiously awaiting the opportunity to put my years of study and psychological knowledge to use. Though the learning was experiential, as we (the students) had all hoped, we left the course with something quite unexpected. From role-play to presentations, we explored various types of counseling methods and theories, but this all paled in comparison to what each of us learned about ourselves through discussions and writing assignments. We laughed, we were engaged, we opened up to one another, and quite a few of us even cried. It was the most profound educational experience of my life.

Ami connected psychological theory with real life experiences to which we could relate. He introduced color and humor to each lecture through subtle jokes and video clips. He brought experiential learning to the table with psychological tests, guest speakers, and role-play. Perhaps it is true that many courses have been designed this way, but there is one more thing: he encouraged and expected each student to apply the material to their own lives (both past and present), resulting in a deeper, more empathetic understanding of human behavior, individual differences, and most important – one's self.

Mary

I chose to write the final entry of my course summary as a letter to Ami; one that explains well the impact of his class on my life, and here it is:

Dear Ami,

It is difficult for me to describe to you how I feel as I finish this assignment. I am accustomed to being awash with relief upon the conclusion of a paper. But this was no ordinary paper. And this is most certainly not a conclusion. Rather, I feel that I am just getting started. I have opened Pandora's Box, and found that it is cluttered with several other boxes. Writing this paper has been therapeutic for me, even in the pages that caused me to revisit pain and unrest. I have explored many issues that I had decided long ago to deny. I have become aware of the depth of work I will have to continue to do in order to resolve my painful past and extinguish its ability to invade my future.

Though I have far to go in my journey for healing, I feel I have done the most difficult part. Rather than avoiding my anguish, which has too often been my response to pain, I have faced my history dead-on and looked my challenges in the face.

In the past, I have had a sense that there are reasons for the chapters of my story. In my bedroom, there is a plaque on the wall that my parents gave to me. It reads: "Your life has a plot; your years have a theme. You can do something in a manner that no one else can" (Max Lucado). For the first time since I hung this on my wall many years ago, I believe these words. I feel sure that my life has a direction and that I am moving forward on my path.

I cannot thank you enough for every single minute that you have touched my life thus far – every moment in the classroom, each email, and especially for this assignment. I feel ready now. I am excited for this next chapter in my life. I cannot wait to become a counselor.

I think the events of my story have a purpose. Beyond making me who I am, my history will grant me the ability to empathize deeply with my clients. Regardless of whether or not I have faced their particular challenge, the range of pain in my life has taught me to be quick to listen and slower to judge.

One more thing that your class has changed in me: for the first time in a very, very long time, I can say that I like who I am. I have been getting re-acquainted with who I am since I began your class, and I have discovered that though I do not particularly like every part of my story, I like its main character. I understand myself better now than when I began your class, and I like who I have uncovered.

Thank you for your wisdom and your wonderfully unconventional methods. Thank you for your trust in who I am and who I can become.

Always,

Mary

Appendix B

How to Make the Most of this Class, or ROPES*

Responsibility

Take personal responsibility for your own learnings.

Openness

Be open to new concepts, new ideas, and new paradigms. Respect other points of view.

Participation

Be involved in the class – practice active listening; share your own opinions and feelings when it feels appropriate.

Experimentation

Experiment with new behavior. For example, if you generally speak up first, practice listening to others. If you seldom self-disclose, consider experimenting with doing that by initiating an interaction.

---

* This is a shorter version of the guide given to me by my colleague, Dr. Dan Ekstein.

SENSITIVITY

Sensitivity, social interest, and basic respect are interrelated. Remember that a particular topic that may not interest you personally may in fact be of high relevance to another student.

Lastly, while learning new ideas, skills, and insights, hopefully we can also have some fun along way.

REFERENCES

Cashdan, S. (1973). *Interactional psychotherapy*. New York, NY: Grune and Stratton.
Clements, A. D. (1995). Experiential-learning activities in undergraduate developmental psychology. *Teaching of Psychology, 22*(2), 115-118.
Cory, G. (1996). *Theory and practice of counseling and psychotherapy*. New York, NY: Brooks/Cole.
Klopfer, W. G. (1974). The seductive patient. In W. G. Klopfer & M. R. Reed (Eds.), *Problems in psychotherapy: An eclectic approach*, (p. 35-46). New York, NY: Wiley.
Kottler, J. A. (2004). *Introduction to therapeutic counselling. (5th edition)*. Toronto, ON: Brooks/Cole.
Kottler, J. A., & Shepard, D. S. (2007). *Introduction to counselling. (6th edition)*. Toronto, ON: Brooks/Cole.
Langs, R. J. (1972). *The therapeutic interaction*. New York, NY: Basic Books.
Langs, R. J. (1988*). A primer of psychotherapy*. New York, NY: Gardner.
Miller, S. (1997). Self-knowledge as an outcome of application journal keeping in social psychology. *Teaching of Psychology, 24*(2), 124-125.
Rokach, A. (1986). Psychotherapy: Close encounters of the intimate kind. *Journal of Contemporary Psychotherapy, 16*(2), 161-182.
Rokach, A. (2007). Causes of loneliness of the physically disabled. *Psychology and Education: An Interdisciplinary Journal, 44*(2), 19-32.
Rokach, A. (2011). From loneliness to belonging: A review. *Psychology Journal, 8*(2), 70-81.
Siegel, B. S. (1991) *Love, medicine & miracles: Lessons learned about self-healing from a surgeon's experience with exceptional patients*. San Francisco, CA: Harper and Row.
Skovholt, T. M., & Ronnestad, M. H. (1995). *The evolving of professional self*. Chichester, UK: Wiley.
Watzlawick, P. (1978). *The language of change*. New York, NY: Norton.

Welch, I. D. (1998). *The path of psychotherapy: Matters of the heart.* New York, NY: Brooks/Cole.

Yalom, I. D. (2002). *The gift of therapy: An open letter to a new generation of therapists and their patients.* New York, NY: HarperCollins.

ABOUT THE AUTHOR

Ami Rokach holds a Ph.D. in psychology from Purdue University. He is the Executive Editor of the *Journal of Psychology: Interdisciplinary and Applied, and* is a clinical psychologist who combines offering individual, couple and sex therapy with teaching and research. Ami is an associate professor and is teaching psychology at The Center for Academic Studies in Israel, and is also a member of the psychology departments at York University in Canada, and Walden University in the USA. His therapeutic and research interests include loneliness, sexuality, couple & sex therapy, anxiety and phobias, traumatic experiences and personal growth, stress management, and palliative care. After 35 years of 'doing' psychology he is still intrigued by human nature, people's suffering, and the real opportunity that we all have to grow, flourish, and reinvent ourselves despite obstacles and painful experiences.

E-mail:arokach@yorku.ca

INDEX

#

21st century, 76

A

Abraham, 21, 86
abuse, 61
academic success, 18
access, 25
acculturation, 76
acquaintance, 66, 81
adjustment, 111
administrators, 7
adults, 108, 113
affirming, 112
age, 14, 20, 54, 55, 73, 75, 76
agoraphobia, 52, 105
alcohol abuse, 70
alienation, 115, 118
American Psychological Association (APA), 10, 41, 54
anesthetics, 49
anger, 51, 80, 114
announcers, 14
antithesis, 68
anxiety, 4, 15, 23, 27, 31, 50, 54, 57, 69, 70, 71, 72, 95, 116
anxiety disorder, 50
appetite, 28
aptitude, 6
assertiveness, 50
assessment, 14, 24, 28
atmosphere, 29, 99, 100, 103
authenticity, 64
authority, 15, 76
awareness, xiv, 49, 50, 96

B

bad habits, 49
base, 18, 35
behavior therapy, 40, 55, 71
behaviors, 5, 25, 49, 51, 64, 74, 75, 90, 91, 97, 106, 107
beneficial effect, 107
benefits, xiii, 75, 100, 114
blame, 51
blood, 15
blood pressure, 15
body weight, v
bones, 60
boredom, 89, 118
brain, 62, 105
budding, 34, 102
burn, 85
burnout, 83

C

calculus, 89
candidates, 22
caricature, 63
catharsis, 93
challenges, 39, 40, 99, 120
childhood, 3, 20, 49, 54, 105, 118
children, 70, 80, 113
Christianity, 40
city, 35
class size, 88
classes, 16, 20, 23, 25, 29, 44, 45, 88, 89, 90, 91, 93, 97, 98, 101, 102, 103, 107, 110, 116
classroom, 88, 90, 91, 92, 100, 102, 103, 115, 117, 119, 120, 121
clients, 14, 28, 29, 34, 41, 48, 49, 51, 52, 53, 57, 59, 60, 61, 64, 66, 69, 72, 73, 74, 76, 77, 78, 79, 81, 82, 83, 86, 92, 96, 102, 110, 111, 112, 113, 114, 115, 121
clinical psychology, 9
clothing, 63
coercion, 75
collaboration, 58
college students, 36
color, 120
combustion, 43
common sense, 65
communication, 68, 99, 115
community, 32, 33, 36, 41, 43
compliance, 106
computer, 6, 10, 81
conception, 69
conference, 20, 32, 33
confidentiality, 46, 59, 67, 77, 102, 110, 119
Confucius, 11
conscious awareness, 111
consciousness, 9, 90
consent, 55
consulting, 5, 39
conviction, 18
counsel, 34
counseling, 29, 35, 44, 89, 90, 91, 92, 93, 97, 102, 103, 104, 106, 107, 108, 109, 111, 112, 113, 116, 117, 118, 119, 120, 125
counseling psychology, 90
country of origin, 76
covering, 106
crabs, 81
creativity, 44, 70
credentials, 76
criminals, 32
critical analysis, 24
criticism, 24
culture, 61
cure, 115
curriculum, 17
customers, 32

D

dance, 82
danger, 82
data collection, 19
data gathering, 67
decay, 47, 50
delegates, 45
demonstrations, xiv, 92, 117
dentist, 49
depression, 27, 83, 114
depth, xiv, 14, 88, 89, 120
destiny, 4
detachment, 89
developmental psychology, 125
diplomacy, 26
disability, 64
disappointment, 104
disclosure, xiii, xiv, 77, 90
discomfort, 58, 74, 82, 95, 97, 112
disorder, 54, 106
dissonance, 62
distress, 5, 106
drawing, 40, 76
dream, 21, 81
dreaming, 50
drug abuse, 83

E

earnings, 52
Eastern Europe, 76
education, 18, 28, 32, 88, 98, 100
educational experience, 120
ego strength, 104
elementary school, 28, 53
emotional experience, 102
emotional responses, 67
empathy, 64, 83, 85, 103, 106, 118, 119
employment, 11, 17, 27, 32, 35
empowerment, 69, 120
encouragement, 67, 119
endorphins, 87
energy, xiv, 61
environment, 45, 102, 114, 115, 117, 119
equality, 94
everyday life, 33, 40, 44, 58, 67, 108
evidence, 119
evolution, 67
examinations, 25
exercise, 5, 95, 107, 108, 112
external locus of control, 77
extraction, 72
extracts, 49

F

facial expression, 117
faith, 86
families, 92
family members, 82
family physician, 104
fear, xiii, 47, 48, 49, 53, 64, 67, 73, 74, 79, 80, 96, 105, 106, 119
feelings, 57, 64, 66, 68, 74, 77, 78, 80, 89, 90, 109, 116, 123
films, 44
financial, 10, 11, 25, 35, 47, 80
fish, 60, 81
flaws, 81
flexibility, 70
flight, xiv, 5
flowers, 47, 71
food, 25
foundations, 116
free choice, 75, 77
freedom, 6, 23, 27, 41, 77
Freud, 35, 75, 76, 81
Freud, Sigmund, 75
friendship, 108, 112
fruits, 72

G

general anesthesia, 76
geography, 25
gifted, 15
God, 3, 63
grades, 4, 10, 17, 18, 19, 20, 22, 27, 29
graduate program, 9, 10, 22, 27, 75
Graduate Record Examination (GRE), 4
grass, 70
Great Britain, 7
growth, 45, 46, 67, 68, 69, 85, 89, 94, 102, 119
guardian, 55
guidance, 109
guidelines, 90
guilty, 52, 111

H

hair, 108
hazards, 82, 83, 85
healing, 48, 78, 92, 103, 110, 115, 117, 118, 120, 125
health, 5
high school, 4, 10, 15, 17, 28, 45, 50, 85, 106
high school grades, 4
historical data, 74
history, 14, 59, 67, 73, 76, 92, 97, 120, 121
homework, 15
honesty, 111
host, 45
hostility, 83

hotel, 26
housing, 17
human, 42, 47, 49, 64, 65, 66, 76, 82, 86, 99, 106, 113, 120
human behavior, 65, 120
human nature, 66
husband, 52, 62, 69, 80

I

ideal, 108
idealism, 83
identification, 83
identity, 14
imagination, 63
immigrants, 76
in vivo, 71
incarceration, 79
income, 6, 52
independence, 83, 92
individual differences, 120
individuals, 89, 100
ineffectiveness, 102
inequality, 58
ingredients, 45
inmates, 51
inner world, 53, 74, 75
insane, 80, 106
insomnia, 70
institutions, 4, 10
intelligence, 18, 23, 55
internalizing, 96
interpersonal skills, 119
intervention, 67
intimacy, 47, 67, 68, 69, 82, 88, 119
intonation, 44
intrinsic value, 89
introspection, 90, 119
irony, 115
isolation, 82, 114, 115
Israel, 4, 9, 13, 58, 127
issues, 3, 11, 33, 46, 48, 51, 53, 54, 59, 64, 68, 70, 74, 77, 80, 81, 95, 105, 113, 116, 119, 120

K

kill, 80

L

learners, 45
learning, xiii, 28, 29, 34, 43, 44, 48, 77, 88, 90, 91, 92, 93, 97, 104, 110, 119, 120, 124, 125
life experiences, 58, 96, 120
light, 10, 19, 21, 114
living conditions, 52
loneliness, 33, 41, 43, 65, 66, 80, 82, 83, 97, 113, 114, 115, 125
long-term memory, 101
love, 20, 30, 43, 48, 68, 69, 78, 102, 114
lying, 5, 106

M

machinery, 15
major issues, 40
majority, 14, 98
malaise, 81
man, 21, 40, 52, 63, 73, 78, 86, 99, 108, 118
marketing, 7
marriage, 54, 60, 61, 70, 73, 76, 78
mass, 98
matter, 27, 45, 63, 74, 101, 102, 112, 117
media, 13
medical, 29, 58, 73
medication, 111
medicine, 4, 125
memorizing, 107
memory, 59, 89, 101, 118
mental activity, 116
mental health, 66, 80, 103, 113
mental health professionals, 66
mentor, 79, 88
merchandise, 51
messages, 57, 74
misuse, 65
motivation, 3, 5, 6, 18, 51, 77, 82

muscles, 24
music, 21, 86, 117

N

needy, 82
neglect, 83
Nelson Mandela, 31, 57
nerve, 26
neutral, 86
Nietzsche, 9, 41, 78
nightmares, 70
North America, 4, 10

O

obstacles, 6, 15, 23, 29, 30, 86, 99
occupational risks, 83
offenders, 54
openness, 93, 102, 110, 119
opt out, 71
optimism, 98
orgasm, 74
outpatient, 27

P

pain, 22, 47, 48, 49, 51, 53, 54, 62, 64, 67, 69, 73, 80, 83, 93, 97, 103, 109, 111, 120, 121
panic attack, 105, 106
parental influence, 11
parenting, 86
parents, 3, 6, 10, 28, 50, 73, 105, 121
participants, 39, 64, 67, 68, 71, 75
peace, 21, 48, 54, 86
permission, 24, 87
perseverance, 15, 26, 30
personal accounts, 40
personal life, 63, 86
personal problems, 50
personal responsibility, 123
personality, 35, 40, 98
phobia, 70, 105, 106

physical abuse, 60
physical activity, 23
physicians, 108
plaque, 121
poetry, 44
politics, 1, 7, 9
population, 18, 54
positive feedback, 43
power inequality, 65
preparation, 24, 45
preparedness, 27
prisoners, 41
private practice, 31, 36, 51, 66, 85
problem solving, 67
professional growth, 34
professional literature, 68
professionals, 24, 28, 104
psychiatrist, 34, 80
psychologist, xiii, 3, 5, 6, 13, 21, 22, 27, 28, 31, 32, 33, 34, 36, 44, 53, 58, 66, 79, 85, 86, 98, 102, 113
psychology, xiii, 3, 4, 5, 6, 9, 10, 11, 13, 14, 16, 18, 20, 21, 23, 28, 29, 32, 33, 34, 35, 42, 43, 45, 47, 65, 79, 85, 87, 92, 100, 106, 110
psychometric exam, 4
psychopathology, 35
psychosocial development, 89
psychotherapy, xiii, 3, 27, 28, 35, 37, 43, 44, 48, 52, 53, 57, 58, 60, 61, 64, 65, 66, 67, 68, 69, 70, 71, 79, 104, 109, 125, 126
publishing, 41
purity, 118

Q

query, 6
questioning, 115

R

race, 45
radio, 14, 79
reactions, 13, 64, 74, 75, 77, 97

reading, xiii, 5, 10, 18, 20, 26, 40, 89, 107
reasoning, 62
recall, 18, 64, 88, 90, 104
recognition, xiv, 100
recovery, 68
regenerate, 24
rejection, 42
relaxation, 23
relevance, 124
relief, 26, 117, 120
requirements, 4, 9, 10, 26, 42, 101, 103
researchers, 39, 40
resistance, 53, 79
resolution, 59
resources, 18, 30
response, 3, 61, 120
risk, 6, 113, 119
role-playing, 112
Roosevelt, Theodore, 3
roots, 58
routines, 90
rowing, 60
rules, 29, 34, 59, 67, 99

S

sadness, 62, 80, 98, 114
safety, xiv, 88, 110, 118, 119
scaling, 28
school, 1, 4, 5, 9, 14, 15, 16, 17, 18, 19, 20, 21, 22, 23, 27, 29, 34, 35, 48, 60, 66, 72, 78, 85, 87, 92, 94, 95, 100, 103, 104, 105, 117
school work, 20
scope, 68
secrete, 87
security, 88, 100, 119
self-awareness, 111
self-confidence, 73
self-control, 82
self-doubt, 83, 115
self-esteem, 4, 18, 50, 71, 105
self-knowledge, 75
self-monitoring, 73
self-reflection, 96

seminars, 35
sex, 28, 35, 73, 74, 78
sexual activity, 74
sexual desire, 61, 73
sexuality, 67
shame, 5, 29, 114
shape, 99
shock, 32, 117
short-term memory, 101
showing, 109
shyness, 40
siblings, 79
signs, 80, 83, 118
snakes, 81
social exchange, 67
social interactions, 66, 112
social life, 17, 24
social psychology, 125
social relations, 65
social skills, 70
social workers, 104
society, 40, 51, 114
speech, 72
spending, 66, 86
sprouting, 28
state, 9, 65, 70, 99
statistics, 19, 34, 97
stimulation, 89
stomach, 62
stress, 23, 76, 82, 83, 85
structure, 34, 110
structuring, 49, 68
style, 41, 45
suicide, 82
supervision, 28, 34, 68, 77, 79
supervisor, vii, 25, 27, 28, 32, 33, 41, 79
sweat, 57

T

talent, 65
target, 26, 111
teachers, 108
teaching experience, 33, 44, 58

techniques, 44, 48, 50, 55, 73, 104, 107, 110, 119
technological advances, 104
teens, 4
teeth, 49
Tel Aviv University, 4, 9
telephone, 63
tension, 23, 25, 108, 109
testosterone, 73
textbook, 45, 89, 93, 108, 109, 115
theoretical approaches, 92, 93
therapeutic approaches, 73
therapeutic encounter, 92
therapeutic process, 76
therapeutic relationship, 48, 64, 65, 67, 68, 72, 104, 107, 108, 109, 110, 112, 113, 114, 115, 116, 119
therapist, xiii, 44, 47, 48, 53, 58, 59, 63, 64, 65, 67, 68, 69, 70, 72, 74, 75, 76, 77, 79, 81, 82, 83, 104, 108, 110, 111, 113, 114, 115, 116, 117, 118
therapy, 14, 28, 35, 36, 44, 46, 47, 48, 50, 51, 52, 53, 54, 57, 58, 60, 61, 62, 63, 64, 65, 66, 67, 68, 70, 71, 72, 73, 74, 75, 77, 78, 79, 80, 81, 82, 83, 85, 86, 92, 102, 104, 107, 108, 109, 110, 111, 113, 116, 118, 126
thoughts, 40, 68, 78, 79, 80, 90, 96, 97, 104
threatening behavior, 82
torture, 103
training, 28, 31, 34, 50, 58, 60, 72, 76, 98
training programs, 31
traits, 83
trajectory, 34
transactions, 40
transference, 75, 108, 110
treatment, 14, 25, 66, 74, 105, 106, 112
treatment methods, 14
trial, 90

U

unconditional positive regard, 64
undergraduate studies, 6, 51, 58, 103
unhappiness, 62
universities, 3, 4, 9, 10, 17, 21, 24, 58
university education, 15
USA, 24

V

variables, 39
vector, 89
vehicles, 106
victims, 51
violence, 60
vomiting, 5
vulnerability, 119

W

waking, 20
walking, 23, 32, 35, 40, 81
war, 41
waste, 100
water, 4
wealth, 85
wear, 111, 117
welfare, 66
well-being, 53, 65
windows, 92
workload, 24
worry, xiii, 116

Y

York University, 9, 33, 43
young adults, 93
young people, 6